More Navy in the News

Navy News
No. 31 DECEMBER, 1956 — Published first Thursday of the month — Price Threepence
SKIDDING TO SAFETY
A flak-damaged Sea Venom of 893 Squadron, H.M.S. Eagle, landing on safely without an undercarriage—November, 1956
DRAFTING FORECAST
Commissioning Programme
PORTSMOUTH — CHATHAM — DEVONPORT
HOME AIR COMMAND
JUDO and JU-JITSU
Order or Renewal Form
"NAVY NEWS" OFFICE, ROYAL NAVAL BARRACKS, PORTSMOUTH
THE ROYAL NAVY AND THE SUEZ CANAL
Full Story of the Operation — See Centre pages

Navy News
The Newspaper of the Royal Navy and Royal Naval Association
No. 180 15th YEAR JUNE, 1969 — Published first Thursday of the month — Price: One Shilling
ROYAL ARRIVAL FOR REVIEW
Pay report this month
TWELVE-MONTH TASK
Forth's 'mutiny' smile
Launching of the Bristol
LONDON'S WARSHIP
Chatham open days on
Parkinson & Partners
Chartered Surveyors & Estate Agents

Navy News
JANUARY 1976 5p
WRENS SET SAIL
FRONT LINE IN ARCTIC
Bulwark gets a reprieve
Nelson tops
Married patch segregation

Navy News
Falklands Task Force
48-PAGE ISSUE
JULY 1982 10p
PRIDE OF A NATION
SHIPS IN BATTLE
SEA HARRIERS REPAY FAITH
Sacrifice
VICTIM
'Mech' title scrapped

NN Navy News
APRIL 1991 20p
'One of the most outstanding campaigns in warfare'
SWEEPING SUCCESS
Cardiff's flag day
Torched!
THE NAVY IN THE GULF
Gulf Medal — and Queen will take the salute

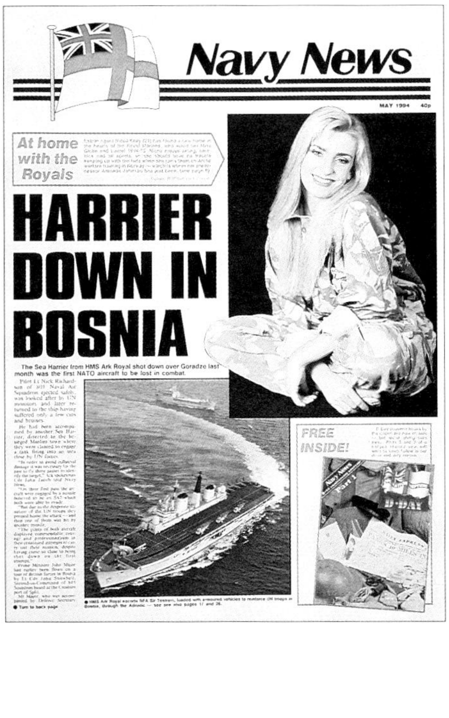
Navy News
MAY 1994 40p
At home with the Royals
HARRIER DOWN IN BOSNIA
FREE INSIDE!

HMS Hermes leads the Falklands Task Force – see page 77.

MORE Navy IN THE News 1954–1994

Jim Allaway

London: HMSO

ST. JAMES'S PALACE

Remarkable though it may seem to some, 40 years have passed since Navy News first appeared. Those years have seen the Royal Navy decrease in size, but its continued success in such latter-day operations as the Falklands, the Gulf and the Adriatic has kept it firmly in the public eye - and recent public opinion polls suggest that the special place the Senior Service has in the hearts of the people who pay for it remains secure.

I know from my travels abroad just how widespread the Navy's influence remains - and how highly it is regarded. Navy News plays a most important part in carrying the message of the Royal Navy's capability, professionalism and good humour to an international readership in all four corners of the globe, and long may it continue to do so.

This timely latest album of "The Navy in the News" serves as a reminder of the range and variety of RN activities that exemplify all that is best in our national character.

Charles

Acknowledgements

Thanks again to Nodge Carnegie and Carol Wardle at HMSO, Norwich for helping put together another album, this time at very short notice; to members of the Royal Navy's Photographic Branch for being "the eyes of the Fleet" in our pages over 40 years; once more, to Beryl Tullett, who for fully half that time has preserved the archive from which this selection is drawn; and to our readers, for their continued support in helping keep the Navy in the News.

Introduction

When 'The Navy in the News' appeared just before Christmas last year, it was suggested that a second volume might be forthcoming, depending on the success of the first. Within a couple of months well over half of the print run had been sold, so HMSO was happy to agree to a follow-up - which neatly coincides with Navy News' 40th birthday.

Albums of old photographs have been hugely popular in recent years, justifying the old maxim that a picture is worth a thousand words.

Navy News has a unique file of the Royal Navy at work over the past four decades – a period that has seen more technological advances than could be encompassed in the same number of centuries.

Today's Navy may be leaner, tauter, trimmer, sharper, sleeker – whichever way you look at it, it is undeniably smaller. However highly effective the surveillance and weapons systems – and personnel – that are packed into the hulls, there are fewer of them to spread around a still considerable number of commitments.

But just about everybody is called upon to do more with less these days and the Navy has had to rise to the challenge along with everyone else.

Last year a national opinion poll showed up a decline in appreciation of a wide range of our national institutions. Practically the sole exception to a sorry tale of disenchantment was the public perception of the record of our Armed Services – and the continuing stream of foreign and Commonwealth students attending the courses they provide suggests that the international regard for their standards and expertise likewise remains undiminished.

National pride is one thing – the resurgence of nationalism in the member states of the old power blocs is something else again. A worrying trend. Beyond its primary role of defending our national security and our interests worldwide the Royal Navy can, now that the superpower competition has receded, look toward playing its part in global policing, in defending threatened minorities. Latterly, in seeking to alleviate the miseries of the civil war in Bosnia, it has taken on more than its fair share.

Public relations, the late Admiral of the Fleet Lord Fieldhouse once famously commented, is the Navy's first line of defence in peacetime, and this year we conducted a readership survey to help us plot the way ahead for Navy News as we approach the next millenium. The response was remarkable. The market research company we engaged told us we would be lucky to receive a thousand replies, based on the size of our circulation. In the first three weeks after publication over 12,000 arrived on our doormat – which is a tremendous tribute to the loyalty and interest of our readers in these times of change.

The overwhelming body of evidence it has provided – which has yet to be fully analysed – already suggests that we have perhaps half a million readers worldwide, representing a wide range of interest and influence.

The very first reply we received came from a retired Army Colonel! A good many of the returns were accompanied by letters – almost all of which made mention of the people to whom subscribers passed their copies on. Naturally, we would rather they bought their own – but we are delighted to know that Navy News has a long shelf life!

One came from a subscriber in a small village in Dorset, who revealed that of the eight people he knew who regularly took Navy News, only two had any sort of naval connection. The current First Sea Lord, on being apprised of this , wondered what the paper contained that could possibly interest them.

Well, we have to cater for a wide range of taste – but hopefully we manage to strike some sort of balance. Something for everyone has always been our ideal.

Another letter came from a former Ministry of Defence employee who until her retirement 15 years ago had been a subscriber. Her nephew renewed her subscription as a Christmas present – and she was pleasantly surprised to find she was still able to find enough material she could relate to.

Perhaps this all reflects, more than anything else, the unique bond the British public feels it has, as a maritime nation, with the Senior Service. It transcends the changing international scene and the country's influence on global affairs – but it helps perpetuate that influence, too.

Even in the short time between the appearance of these two albums the Navy has seen momentous changes. If these have been largely dictated by economic considerations, they have nevertheless wonderfully concentrated the minds of naval planners...

Three classes of warships have departed from the scene. We have seen the last of the Leanders – surely the most successful of all the RN's post World War II designs; most of the Type 21 frigates, which suffered tragic losses in the Falklands War; and of the Ton Class minesweepers, last of the Navy's wooden walls' that have given outstanding service for 40 years.

Soon we will see the removal of the new Upholder Class conventional submarines whose role in defending the Faroes/Iceland gap became redundant with the end of the Cold War.

The end of 1993 also saw the demise of the WRNS as a separate arm of the Naval Service. The advent of women at sea at once made its continuance an anachronism but the speed with which its disbandment was made possible was even so a tribute to the adaptability of the Wrens to what had hitherto been an alien environment.

So many departures ... I have long been worried that Navy News might rely too heavily on the support of 'hostilities only' veterans. Inevitably, more and more of these are now 'crossing the bar' – But our circulation has remained remarkably buoyant over the past dozen or so years, during which time we expected a decline through 'natural wastage' and a 25 per cent reduction in the serving strength.

So we are obviously drawing in new readers. Perhaps this is a reflection of the increasing trend towards shorter term careers in the RN. Maybe those who return to civvy street soon start remembering their days with the Senior Service with affection – and turn to Navy News to renew their ties with their most formative years.

Navy News is also the newspaper of the Royal Naval Association. It is a popular misconception that membership of the RNA has lately declined. Some branches have been forced to close through lack of support – but others are still being formed, both at home and overseas. And the truth is that membership has nearly doubled over the past decade or so.

Tugg Willson's 'Jack' cartoon character has done much to help Navy News keep in tune with our changing times.

This time I have chosen one of Tugg's perennial themes to accompany the selection of photographs and stories offered here – the writing of letters home.

'Jack' has always had trouble with his correspondence. He looks forward to getting his mail, but he's not much of a scribe himself – and most of his effort goes into inventing excuses for *not* putting pen to paper.

His future biographers may find a problem here. Letter writing is a dying art in the age of the telephone and the video recorder – and the durability of video tapes and modern colour snapshots is lately being questioned, too.

People don't keep letters anymore either – gone are the days when every note from a loved one was tied up in a bundle with pink ribbon and packed away for posterity.

The researchers who have been tasked with putting the events of fifty years ago into perspective have been able to draw on a wealth of original source material – much of it coming from personal reminiscences set down pretty much at the time the events they describe took place.

Navy News this year made an appeal for D-Day memories with a view to compiling its own retrospective – and was rewarded with an avalanche of pin-sharp recollections that give the lie to the old adage that old men forget.

All the World War II anniversaries that have crowded in upon us have brought an enormous increase in our mailbag – from professional historians, amateur researchers and readers who simply wish to impart a few lines of reminiscence. Many remarkable reunions of old shipmates, out of touch for half a century or more, have thereby been effected – from all points of the compass.

On the basis of the evidence we have lately received, I see no reason why this trend should not continue – and allow Navy News to extend its appeal into the next millenium.

Certainly, the Navy has been hitting the headlines with a vengeance in the first half of the Nineties. We can confidently predict that it will carry on doing so during the rest of this uniquely challenging decade – now that it has rationalised its resources to provide the United Kingdom with the most modern Fleet it has had since the 1920s.

Jim Allaway
Editor, Navy News
HMS Nelson
June, 1994

First published 1994

ISBN 0 11 772802 0

Also available from HMSO

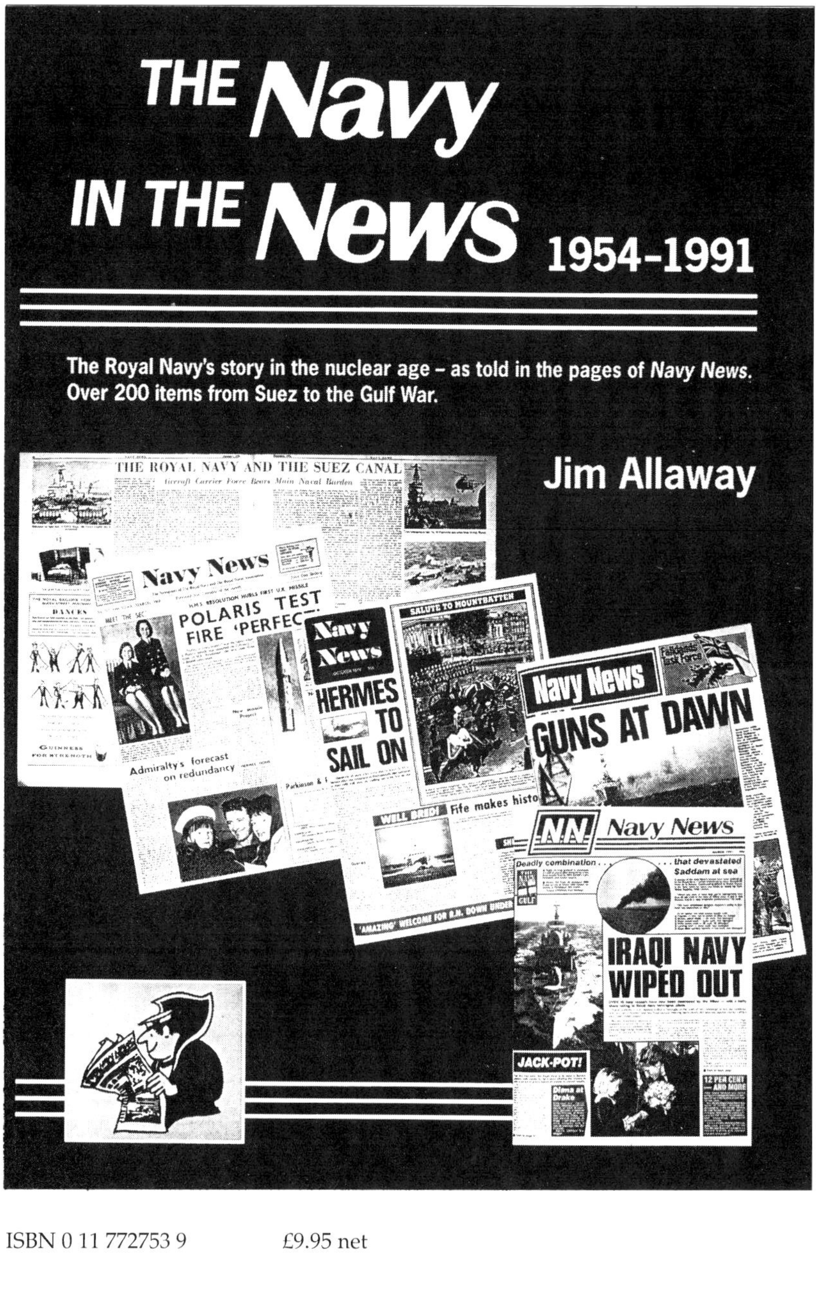

"Jim Allaway has produced a book that should interest even non-Navy buffs. He's done this by some excellent editing that has kept the items short and sharp . . . *The Navy in the News* contains more pictures than most books of the genre"

British Association of Industrial Editors Editing for Industry Awards 1994

Since it first entered the BAIE competition in 1972, Navy News has won 65 awards without missing a single year – a unique achievement.

ISBN 0 11 772753 9 £9.95 net

Navy News

FORTY YEARS ON

1 *Passing for Thermopylae*

The conversion of HM submarine Thermopylae was so revolutionary that few observers would afterward be able to recognise one of the World War II T-class boats. This one, built at Chatham, had in fact commissioned just too late for active service in September 1945. For the next five years she served with the Fleet before returning to Chatham for extensive modernisation and reconstruction which included the latest type of 'snort' equipment, radar and offensive weapons.

The past two years had seen her almost exclusively engaged in trials. Other boats of the class that had been similarly brought up to date included Taciturn, Tiptoe, Turpin, Truncheon and Totem. [*August 1954*]

1

2 *Little bird flies home*

The return of HMS Wren after eight years' service in foreign waters was a memorable occasion for the WRNS. The frigate was launched on 11 August 1942 by Dame Vera Laughton Matthews, then Director WRNS – and she was there on the jetty at Portsmouth to welcome her home.

While the ship was under construction a voluntary collection was made by the Wrens which produced over £4,000 towards the cost of building – a tidy sum in those days. The cost of the Sick Bay equipment was subscribed to by the relatives and friends of the 22 Wrens whose lives were lost when the SS Aguila was torpedoed and sunk on passage to Gibraltar on 19 August, 1941. A plaque in their memory was set above the Sick Bay door. [*February 1955*]

2

3 *Wrangler leads out of Malta*

HMS Wrangler, leader of the Fifth Frigate Squadron, leaves Malta for the UK to recommission for further service with Whirlwind, Roebuck and Wakeful. [*June 1955*]

3

4

4 *Indus-trial for First Eleven*

Centrepiece of a celebration of the Golden Jubilee of the Navy's Mechanician Branch was this picture of HMS Indus – training ship at Devonport from 1906 and 1910, when the first class of Mechanicians qualified to sit for the examination of Warrant Mechanician. Out of 16, eleven were successful and five were promoted in November 1910 – the remaining six later. They were thus the first Stokers to become Officers. [*October 1955*]

5

6

5 *Theseus's heroic effort*

Introducing the "Ships of the Royal Navy" portrait series was HMS Theseus, the 13,350 ton light fleet carrier completed in 1946, which was then flying the flag of Rear Admiral H W Biggs, commander of the Home Fleet Training Squadron at Portland. She is seen here out of Portsmouth, lined with men of the 16th Independent Parachute Brigade Group and carrying all their equipment and transport. – Photo: Associated Press [*October 1955*]

6 *Brum beats the drum*

When the luxury cruise liner Caronia visited Malta, the cruiser HMS Birmingham decorated Grand Harbour with equal panache. [*October 1955*]

7

8

9

7 *Thai link for two*

The cruiser HMS Newfoundland and the destroyer HMS Comus alongside at Bangkok, Thailand after taking part in exercise Firm Link, a three-day SEATO effort that included sea and air units of several nations. The Newfoundland was flying the flag of the Flag Officer Second-in-Command Far East Station Vice Admiral R. F. Elkins, leading a force that also included the destroyer HMS Consort, the Australian destroyers Anzac and Tobruk and the New Zealand frigate Pukaki. They had carried out air/sea rescue duties during a helicopter troop lift between the US aircraft carrier Princeton and Bangkok airport. [*April 1956*]

8 *Saturday Night Out*

Using a new miniature TV camera for the first time, the BBC transmitted vision and sound from a submarine, HMS Tapir, via HMS Grenville (seen here) – which had to keep directional aerials trained on the submarine and the receiving station at St Catherine's Point on the Isle of Wight throughout the broadcast. No easy task in a ship which was under helm most of the time . . .

'Saturday Night Out' – also picked up by viewers in Belgium and France – featured a mock attack on a surface ship in the Channel in this pioneering piece of Navy PR narrated by Richard Dimbleby [*July 1956*]

10

9 *Lynx, first of the Leopards*

Launched by the Princess Royal – the sister of King George VI – on January 12, 1955, HMS Lynx was the first of the Leopard Class frigates to complete. Designed primarily for the protection of convoys from aircraft attack and as a small type of destroyer for offensive operations, she was armed with four 4.5 inch guns, two smaller guns and the Squid anti-submarine mortar. [*April 1957*]

10 *Booties' Baby*

HMS Loch Killisport, an anti-submarine frigate specially refitted for operations in the Persian Gulf and the East Indies station, sailed for the Gulf on August 15. She had a detachment of Royal Marines on board – the first to be embarked in frigates in lieu of seamen. Sea service of Royal Marines had hitherto been restricted to ships the size of cruisers and above. [*August 1956*]

11 *Spires of steel*

HMS Salisbury, the first of a new class of vessels named after cathedral cities, was an aircraft direction frigate. Her role was to act as a picket stationed ahead of fleet or convoy to give early warning of any aircraft threat. In 1959, in company with HMS Tenby, she entered Lake Erie for the first visit there by RN ships since the War of Independence. She later became the last ship to carry out the Beira Patrol, enforcing sanctions against Rhodesia after its unilateral declaration of independence. [*September 1957*]

11

12 **Plover laid 10,000 eggs**

Twenty-one years in commission and still going strong – HMS Plover, the coastal minesweeper that first came into service in 1937, had never paid off. She laid over 10,000 mines during the war years and in a letter written in November 1944 their Lordships stated: ". . . the method in which these operations were successfully completed . . . reflects greatly on all concerned. The work of the ship has been marked throughout by its persistent accuracy and freedom of breakdown." [*April 1958*]

12

13

13 **Exploring the deep at speed**

Based on the Third Submarine Squadron at Faslane on the Clyde, HMS Explorer – with her sister Excalibur reputedly the fastest submarine in the word, logging over 25 knots submerged – was engaged in detailed analysis of very high underwater speeds to gain experience in the new techniques and drills which would soon emerge with the advent of the RN's first nuclear boat, HMS Dreadnought. As a change from this work, she would occasionally provide target services for surface anti-submarine forces operating out of Londonderry. [*April 1958*]

14 *Last of the wrecking crew*

HMS Steepholm, sole survivor of the 18 Isles Class trawlers that once formed the Wreck Dispersal Fleet commissioned at the end of World War II to clear 500 charted wrecks from around the shores of the UK. The work was now largely complete and due to be taken over by the Lighthouse Authorities and Harbour Boards – a return to the situation existing prior to 1939. Based at Chatham and mainly occupied on wrecks around the East and South coasts, the Steepholm was built in 1943 and started her career as a wreck dispersal vessel in December 1945 after conversion from an anti-submarine trawler. Wrecks were dispersed – or preferably buried – using Mk VII depth charges. [*June 1958*]

14

15

15 *Cumberland closes with few gaps*

The veteran cruiser HMS Cumberland, then the oldest sea-going ship in the Navy, leaves Malta for her birthplace at Barrow-in-Furness at the end of a distinguished career. Very few warships had attained the distinction of being in full commission after 30 years' active service. The only breaks were for modernisation in 1935-36 and a short period in reserve from 1947-49. Most famous of her actions was the Battle of the River Plate – but other battle honours included Arctic 1942-43, North Africa 1942, Sabang 1944 and Burma 1945. In recent years she had been a trials cruiser, giving exhaustive tests to the new 3 inch and 6 inch fully automatic guns developed by Vickers Armstrong. She also undertook "pre-wetting" trials against radio-active fallout. [*November 1958*]

16

16 *Seaside special sea-rider*

HMS Torquay, turning at speed during exercises, was the first of the hugely successful Whitby Class anti-submarine frigates launched in 1954 at Harland and Wolff's Belfast yard by Lady Monckton.

Sixteen of the class were all named after seaside resorts. With her high focsle and clean lines anticipating the Leanders, she rode well in a seaway and was exceptionally dry. The operations room was said at the time to be the finest ever put into a small ship. Extensively modernised in 1971, she was the first ship to be fitted with a modern computer-activated action information system which later became standard. [*January 1959*]

17

18

20

17 Dawn breeze over the Rock

This fine picture taken from the carrier HMS Victorious, as HMS Gambia leaves Gibraltar to take part in Exercise Dawn Breeze, shows how the clouds from the Mediterranean side are swept up and over the Rock, producing the familiar Levante. The Fiji Class cruiser had come out of refit at Rosyth the previous November and made her first foreign visit to Vigo. Launched in 1940, she was on loan to the Royal New Zealand Navy from 1943-46 and represented New Zealand at the surrender of Japan. She was scrapped in 1968 after service as the flagship of the Flag Officer Second in Command Mediterranean and First Cruiser Squadron and of the Commander-in-Chief East Indies. [*May 1959*]

18 Hot work for Centaur

HMS Centaur at speed during hot weather trials in the Persian Gulf – this was the first time an aircraft carrier had operated in this area in mid-summer. [*August 1959*]

19 Seahawks and Sea Demon

Seahawks of 804 Squadron start up on board HMS Albion during the SEATO Exercise 'Sea Demon' in the China Sea. [*September 1959*]

20 All the fun of the fair

Japanese children enjoy a party in HMS Ceylon, visiting Yokohama with a roundabout and aerial ride rigged on the fo'c'sle. The cruiser had taken part in SEATO exercises with American, Australian, New Zealand and French ships which ended in Manila before cleaning and paint ship in Hong Kong

19

to prepare for a United Nations Command cruise to Korea and Japan.

In Korea a few of the ship's company were able to inspect the neutral zone at Panmunjon – where they were impressed by the enormous size of the South Korean Army, then the fifth largest in the world.

The Ceylon was also kept busy in the annual exercise JET in the Indian Ocean, this year involving the Royal Australian Navy, Royal New Zealand Navy, Royal Ceylon Navy, and the Indian and Pakistan Navies. The six week period included calls at Colombo, Cochin, Karachi and Trincomalee. [*October 1959*]

21

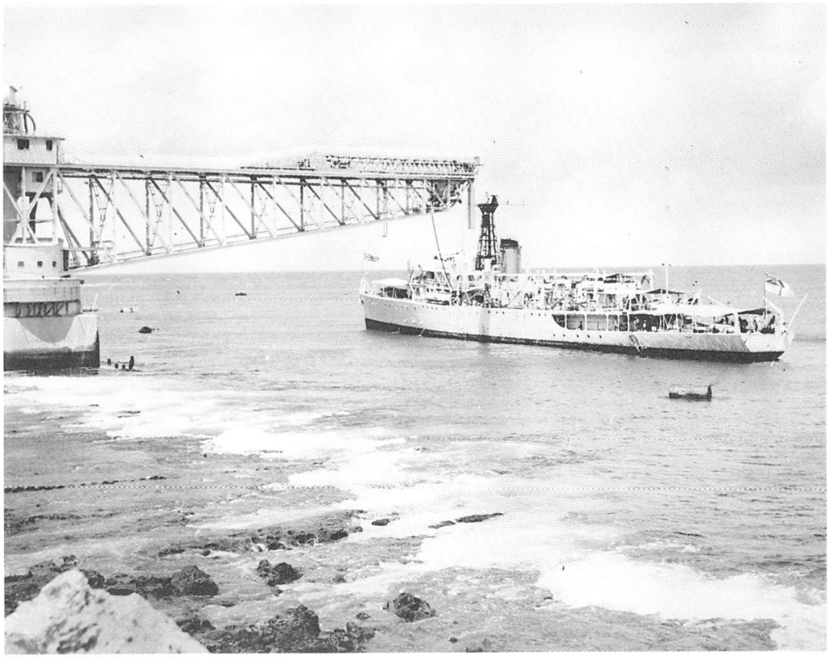

21 **Cook's tour of discoveries**

The survey ship HMS Cook was retracing the steps of her famous namesake Captain Cook in the South Pacific, visiting the Solomon Islands, Suva, Fiji and the Gilberts. She is seen under the cantilever at Ocean Island. [*November 1959*]

22

22 Shackleton steams south through the Menai Strait

"A superb piece of seamanship" was how a former chief pilot of the Menai Strait described HMS Shackleton's careful negotiation of the 14 mile strip of water that separates Anglesey from the Welsh mainland.

After months of survey work off the west coast of Scotland and North Wales, Lieut.-Cdr W J L Smith DSO, RNZN decided on an unusual route home to Chatham. It is rare for vessels of over 100 tons to make the passage and as the Shackleton displaced 830 tons the attempt excited a lot of media attention.

With conditions favourable over the Caernarvon Bar and little or no wind in the Strait itself, the passage was completed without incident, however. [*January 1960*]
Picture: Daily Express

23

24

23 **Feline grace of the last of the cats**

HMS Jaguar, seen here on her trials, the last of the "Cat" Class anti-submarine frigates, was commissioned at the Clydeside yards of Denny Bros. All four were allocated for service on the South Africa and South America station. [*January 1960*]

25

24 **Bulwark keeps cool east of Suez**

HMS Bulwark was the first all-helicopter commando carrier to be commissioned. Later based at Singapore, she was designed for operations east of Suez.

"The primary job of the ship in the Cold War is likely to be extinguishing the brush fire before it can spread. In limited wars of all kinds HMS Bulwark will provide a highly amphibious force . . . She may well act as a striking force to secure a beach and the immediate hinterland in order that the main force can land."

The ship was fitted with the most extensive air conditioning system in the Navy at this time to improve habitability in tropical climates. [*January 1960*]

25 **Rousing reception in the Land of the Rising Sun**

HMS Crane had seen action off Okinawa in 1945 and later Korea, but now she was revisiting old haunts on a mission of goodwill. After sailing from Hong Kong in company with units of the Far East Fleet, hands were closed up at action stations when passing through the Formosa Strait – but there was a warm welcome at Chinhae, the "Korean Riviera", where a party for 150 orphans ended with the children staging a dance in traditional dress.

Later the Crane and HMS Cardigan Bay entered the Japanese Inland Sea at Nichiyama on passage to Yokohama and Kobe. Great crowds lined the narrows of the northern entrance heralding "a tremendous whirl of entertainment". Nagoya was the next port of call and here the reception given the Crane – the only warship present – was in traditional geisha style.

Japan was voted "a splendid run ashore" by the Black Swan class frigate – but very expensive. The extent of the post-war Japanese economic miracle was already apparent.

HMS Crane, originally a sloop, was first commissioned in 1943 and took part in the invasion of Sicily in July that year. Until the Normandy landings, in which she took part, she was employed on convoy duties, carrying out offensive anti-submarine patrols. She joined the British Pacific Fleet at the beginning of 1945. Paid off into reserve at the end of 1946, she was recommissioned in August 1951 for service in the Far East and had since steamed over 30,000 miles. [*August 1960*]

26 Owen's first footing

The first recorded landing on the barren Brazilian islands of Martin Vaz in the South Atlantic was made by HMS Owen, pictured here shortly before at Tristan da Cunha. The survey ship was on her way to undertake hydrographic work in South Georgia.

The three small islets of the group are situated about 650 miles east north east of Rio de Janeiro and are described in navigation manuals as "steep and inaccessible" – yet a small party from the ship, including a number of civilian scientists, succeeded in leaping ashore on the largest of the trio. An officer and a rating scaled its 300 ft peak while others collected botanical, biological and geological specimens.

When the Owen had arrived at Tristan – Britain's "loneliest colony" – it was discovered that the island's 270 inhabitants were without a doctor. The ship's medical officer, Surgeon Lieutenant R S McKinnon, was put ashore for a month to attend to their medical needs. Later in the year the islanders would value the Royal Navy's assistance as never before. [*January 1961*]

26

27

27 Blackpool towers Fujiyama

The first nine months of 1961 kept HMS Blackpool at sea for 134 days, steaming 48,452 miles in duties that took her from Iceland to Japan with 21 days on patrol in the Persian Gulf during the Kuwait crisis in July. A fortnight on fishery protection duties kicked off the second half of her General Service Commission. Then, after landing arctic clothing at Devonport, she sailed for Singapore via Capetown, Mombasa and Aden.

After calling at Hong Kong, she departed for Japan, was the first RN ship to visit the port of Miyasu since 1924, and paid visits to Muroran and Yokohama – whence an intrepid Outward Bound party travelled to Mount Fujiyama and succeeded in scaling the sacred mountain's snow-capped summit. On the way back to Singapore the ship took part in fleet exercises and was looking forward to a visit to Australia in August – but troubles in Kuwait intervened. [*November 1961*]

28 Going Forth cocks a snoot

"A submarine depot ship conjures up visions of weeks and months spent alongside, or swinging round the buoy, but HMS Forth" (pictured here with four British submarines alongside at the Norfolk, Virginia naval base) "can cock a snoot at all who regard her as always sitting on piles of gin bottles and corned beef tins. . ."

Having arrived back in the United Kingdom a year before after 12 years' continuous commission in the Mediterranean, she went on to visit Brest and Hamburg, embarked the Flag Officer Submarines from Devonport to Portsmouth to attend the celebrations attending the award of the Freedom of the Borough of Gosport to the Submarine Service, and supported the Second Submarine Squadron in an extensive submarine exercise with the United States Navy. [*November 1961*]

28

29 First frigate with a flight

HMS Ashanti, the first of the new Tribal class of general purpose frigates to come into service, was accepted from the Glasgow shipyard of Yarrow and Co Ltd on November 23. For the first time, a helicopter – a Westland Wasp operating in an anti-submarine role from a small flight deck fitted aft – was carried as an integral part of a frigate's armament. With the addition of two 4.5 inch and a pair of 40mm Bofors anti-aircraft guns, a Limbo three-barrelled depth bomb mortar and two Seacat close range ship-to-air guided missile launchers, she was capable of meeting the main escort functions of anti-submarine protection, anti-aircraft defence and aircraft direction. A steam turbine was used for normal cruising with a gas turbine providing additional boost power at high speeds and an ability to get under way quickly in an emergency without having to wait for steam to be raised. [*December 1961*]

29

30 Oberon a dream boat

HMS Oberon, 'Ship of the Royal Navy' No 74, was the name boat – submarines are 'boats', not 'ships' – of a hugely successful class of post-war conventional diesel-electric submarines that were to give sterling service right up to the Gulf War of 1991 and beyond. In their time they were rated as the best in the world, being employed by the navies of Australia, Canada, Brazil, and Chile as well as by the Royal Navy. Practically repeat editions of the Porpoise class, they were capable of high underwater speeds in any part of the world and were equipped to fire homing torpedoes. Since this photograph was taken, the pennant numbers of submarines were changed to enable all the post-1945 conventional boats to bear numbers from S 01 onwards. Oberon's new pennant number was S 09. [*January 1962*]

30

31 Switchback Cat's commission

HMS Lynx, the Type 41 anti-aircraft frigate of the Leopard Class seen here off Cape Point, came into Portsmouth for a 48-hour stopover before going on to Chatham to pay off. The third commission of this Home South Atlantic and South America Station ship had been outstandingly successful although her programme had borne little relation to that envisaged when she commissioned at Portsmouth in February, 1960. The ship left for the South Atlantic three months before the intended date and instead of doing a full year on that station, she was detached to the West Indies for the last four months. Lynx returned to the Home Fleet in August, 1961 only to be sent off to the West Indies, arriving on January 2. During this commission she travelled over 70,000 miles and visited 50 different ports and 25 countries. [*February 1962*]

32 Murray rolls the other side of the coin

"Sandy beaches, waving palms and dusky maidens play a part in the travels of HM ships, but there is another side." HMS Murray is seen here rolling through an Atlantic gale during a recent NATO exercise. [*February 1962*]

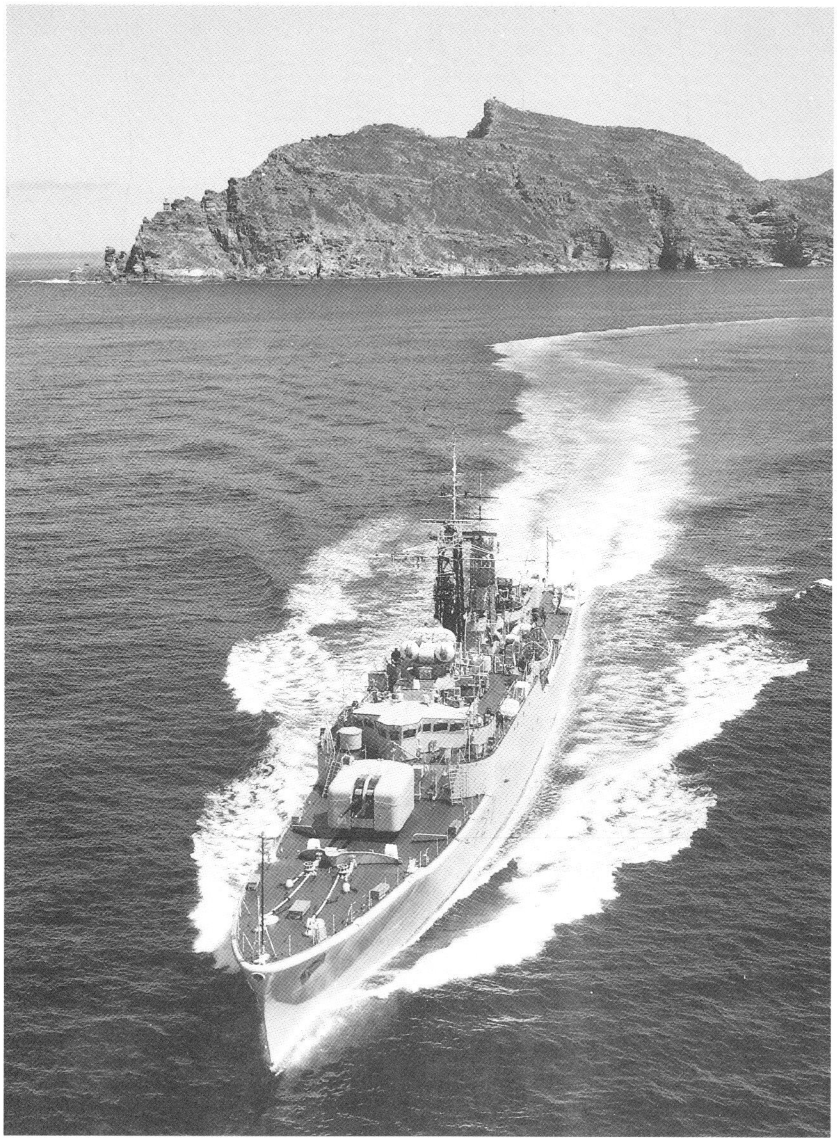

31

32

33

33 *Swan song out of Singapore*

Seen here leaving Singapore on the last journey of her eventful career is the 24-year-old cruiser HMS Belfast – on her way home to join the Fleet Reserve. Belfast was commissioned just before World War II and three months after completion was mined in the Forth, necessitating almost complete reconstruction. Among her wartime tasks she provided cover for convoys to Russia, took part in the Scharnhorst action and supported the Army in the capture of Caen. During the Korean War Belfast steamed 82,500 miles on the Far East Station, where she spent most of the rest of her post-war days. [*May 1962*]

34

35

34, 35 *Meon and Messina – beach mastery at Kuwait*

HMS Meon (Landing Ship Headquarters) and HMS Messina (Landing Ship Tanks) were two key units of the Amphibious Warfare Squadron, whose role in the Kuwait crisis had provided a graphic illustration of the value of a small, highly mobile force of landing ships which had been underlined by the D-Day operations – likely to remain the largest amphibious undertaking of all time.

During the Kuwait operation large numbers of tanks, vehicles and stores were landed in answer to a call for help from the Sheikh – under the control of the headquarters ship with her large array of radio equipment. The LSTs were capable of carrying quantities of tanks as well as up to eight assault landing craft to carry troops or marines to the beach to initiate the attack.

"As the LST with its load of Centurion tanks moves into the beach, it drops a kedge anchor over its stern when it is just short. It will use this to pull itself off after the tanks have landed. As the beach is approached the heavy steel doors are opened and the ramp over which the tanks pass is made ready for lowering. When the ship finally grounds the ramp is lowered and the tanks slowly rumble forward to go ashore.

"It is vitally important that the water gap between the ship and the shore is not too deep as a tank will flood in water more than about four feet deep. The first tank ashore is watched with a certain amount of apprehension, because if she gets stuck the whole operation will be delayed and possibly fail. If the beach consists of soft sand, a steel mesh roadway is laid from the ship's ramp to firm ground and this work is done manually by members of the Beachmaster's team ..." [*June 1962*]

36

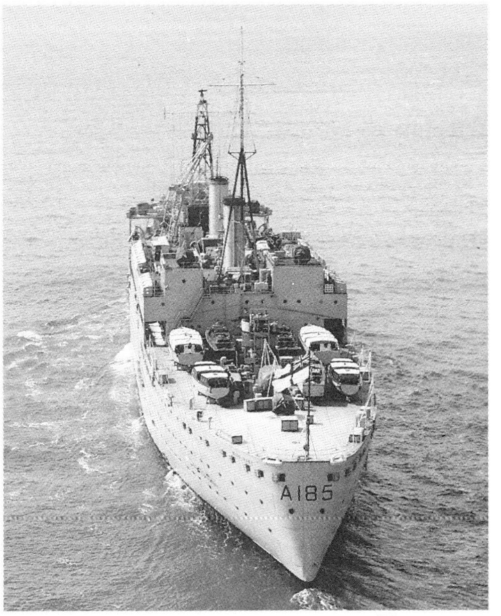

38

36 **Buoyant baby boomer**

HMS Layburn, one of the two 'Lay' Class of boom-defence vessels designed and built since World War II, completed on July 7, 1960. As well as minor salvage work and the towing of net sections, she could lay and maintain the latest types of underwater and surface boom defences, first-class moorings and navigational buoys. [*July 1962*]

37 **Radiant in white**

With the jet blast deflector in position, a Royal Navy Buccaneer, dressed in her anti-radiation white coat, is poised on a catapult on board HMS Hermes, ready for takeoff. [*July 1962*]

38 **Nice to come home to!**

HMS Maidstone, the 12,700 ton submarine depot ship had been converted and modernised at Portsmouth to look after Britain's first nuclear submarine, HMS Dreadnought. Equipped with laundry, canteens, bakery and cinema, she could see to the needs of up to nine operational boats. [*August 1962*]

37

40

40 *Alert to the forces of peace*

HMS Alert – the Flag Frigate of the Far East Station, which consisted roughly of the eastern half of the Indian Ocean north of 10 degrees South and the western half of the Pacific Ocean north of the Equator. Admiral Sir David Luce, Commander-in-Chief Far East Station, noted: "Over the past years the Far East Fleet has been growing steadily in numbers and in strength, but more important is the steady flow of new and modernised ships of all classes to the station. The Far East Fleet is one of the most potent forces for peace in this part of the world and will long remain so."

In the 'Year of the Tiger' HMS Tiger was by happy coincidence with the Far East Fleet – along with the Navy's strike carrier East of Suez, HMS Ark Royal; the 8th Destroyer Squadron; the 3rd Frigate Squadron; the 104th Minesweeping Squadron, associated recently with anti-piracy patrols off north-east Borneo; the 1st and 4th Frigate Squadrons; and the 7th Submarine Division, which ranged over vast distances from Japan to Australia and westward to India and Ceylon. [*October 1962*]

'ERE! MASTERMIND – 'OWJA SPELL ETERNALLY ?
L-I-A-R

39 *Lionised at Guzz and Gozo*

HMS Lion was open to visitors at Plymouth Navy Days. Here she leaves Pietta, Malta, to take part in an exercise in the Mediterranean. Lion had recently commissioned at Devonport for service at home, the Mediterranean and East of Suez. [*August 1962*]

39

41

41 *Dreadnought exceeds expectations*

HMS Dreadnought, the Royal Navy's first nuclear-powered submarine, was on her trials. The second HMS Valiant – an all-British design – was under construction, with the third, HMS Warspite ordered.

The latter pair were to use reactors based on the Royal Navy's prototype developed at Dounreay in Scotland. Meanwhile Dreadnought had exceeded her expected surface speed.

The current Flag Officer Submarines, Rear Admiral Hugh Mackenzie, had just been selected as Chief Polaris Executive following the historic Nassau Agreement between President Kennedy and Prime Minister Macmillan that transferred the wielding of the nuclear deterrent from the Royal Air Force to the Royal Navy. Mackenzie, wartime commander of one of the most successful British submarines of the Second World War, HMS Thrasher, whose officers and men won two VC's, a DSO, two DSCs and six DSMs and sank 40,000 tons of enemy shipping, had long advocated the adoption of the Polaris missile in British submarines, with a home-built warhead under British control. The keels of the boats were to be laid the following year with the first coming into service in 1968. [*February 1963*]

42 Devonshire cream of the County Class

HMS Devonshire, first of the six County Class guided missile destroyers – Hampshire, Kent and London were expected to join the Fleet in this year and good progress was being made with the other two, Fife and Glamorgan. These were to carry the Seaslug Mk 2 later to be fitted to the other four. For the time being they carried the Seaslug Mk 1 medium range ship-to-air guided missile. Short-range anti-aircraft Seacat missiles were also part of the armament of these powerful ships. [*March 1963*]

43 Full frontal for Otter

An unusual bows-on photograph of the Oberon Class submarine HMS Otter. Compare with HMS Ocelot on page 99. [*March 1963*]

42

43

44 Lion's share of rescue missions

What was "possibly one of the longest salvage tows recorded by a ship of the Royal Navy in peacetime" fell to the cruiser HMS Lion – seen here as guard ship for the Regatta at Trincomalee after hauling the Indonesian merchantman Blewah 480 miles to Aden.

The Lion had first encountered Blewah lying hove to across the Red Sea. She reported that she had been floating for three days with engine failure – but did not require assistance. Four hours later, however, she was heard on the distress frequency and the cruiser turned back 40 miles and sent over a boarding party. They learned that Blewah was a new ship, an 840 ton cargo vessel built in Yugoslavia and on route for Djakarta. There was little prospect of getting her diesel engines going again so the long pull began into a strong wind, which deteriorated into a Force 7 and parted the towing shackle. Once the cable was secured again speed was reduced to three knots and it was over three and a half days before they came into port – the crew of a passing Russian merchantman eyeing askance "the sight of an Indonesian cargo vessel in tow by an HM ship".

The Blewah's crew's diet consisted almost entirely of rice. "As the boarding party found this fare rather dull and its method of preparation somewhat rustic, a stretcher loaded with stores and provisions (including, of course, the rum ration) had been floated from Lion to Blewah each day."

A few weeks later, on sailing from Hong Kong to Saigon, the Lion responded to another distress call. The Panamanian ship National Glory was

44

on fire 200 miles away and had been abandoned by her crew, most of whom had been rescued. But six were still missing, believed to be adrift in a lifeboat and the cruiser joined in the search. Able Seaman Raymond Smith, keeping lookout through powerful binoculars, sighted a white speck in the sea about six miles away. The half dozen Chinese survivors were discovered in a waterlogged boat, without food or water, and surrounded by sharks. "Two days later six very grateful Chinese were landed in Saigon from where they returned to Hong Kong by air." [*April 1963*]

45 **Motherly Manxman**

In a month when the development of Faslane on the Clyde as the future base for the Polaris submarine fleet was announced by Lord Carrington – then First Lord of the Admiralty – HMS Manxman was an echo of the past, revived for a new role at the cost of £1m. Built between 1930 and 1941 as a fast minelayer, she had been newly commissioned at Chatham as a forward support ship for coastal minesweepers. She would act as mothership to a squadron of these who, with her enlarged capacity for storing food and supplies and her ability to transfer them underway, would be able to remain at sea independent of base assistance for long periods. [*May 1963*]

45

46 **Auriga at Argentia**

HM Submarine Auriga of the 6th Submarine Division, operating with the Royal Canadian Navy out of Halifax, Nova Scotia, arrives at the US Naval Base at Argentia, Newfoundland. [*May 1963*]

46

47 *Cutting encounter for Cambrian*

"She shall have music wherever she goes..." HMS Ursa, a Type 15 fast anti-submarine frigate built at Woolston in 1944 as a destroyer and converted at Hebburn in 1954, became the first Royal Navy ship to have Reditune music installed – 100 endless tapes ranging from light classics to the latest hits comprising over 4,000 titles. Her commanding officer commented: "The service has proved to be a very effective and pleasing means of increasing efficiency..."

● This photograph was taken from the deck of HMS Cambrian. For some reason the officer in the whole of the foreground of the picture was later excised and the rest brilliantly retouched to show Ursa steaming apparently alone. Perhaps it was felt the clean lines of the young Commander posing by the signal lamp detracted from those of Ursa, then on her way to a commission in the Caribbean! [*July 1963*]

47

48 *Submariners' strange salt lake sighting*

A party from HMS Tabard – the first RN submarine to commission in Australia at the end of a long refit at Sydney's Cockatoo Island dockyard – discovered a group of mysterious aboriginal cave drawings when they undertook a biological survey near a remote salt lake, 200 miles south west of Alice Springs. Crudely drawn human figures and a spoked wheel decorated the walls, bones littered the floor and there was evidence of some very old fireplaces . . .

Four officers and four ratings from the Fourth Submarine Division took part in the 15-day, 4,500 mile expedition directed by the Australia Museum to survey the lake, so isolated that it was believed animals living there might have evolved differently from other Australian species. [*December 1963*]

48

49

49 *Cooking with gas at 120°F*

The first of the 'Tribals', HMS Ashanti, was the first major warship of the Royal Navy powered with gas turbines to have completed a General Service Commission. She had spent the past 10 months serving in the Persian Gulf and Arabian Sea. "Many Arab rulers who have visited the ship have been most impressed that Britain has sent one of her most modern frigates to the area. "On many occasions Cdr Hepworth and sometimes his officers and chief petty officers have paid return visits to rulers' palaces. Despite the complex etiquette involved on these occasions, such as always eating with the right hand, no diplomatic errors were made by any of the ship's company . . . "During a visit to Karachi the ship's rugby football team beat Karachi City by six points to nil – the first time the local team had been beaten by a visiting warship."

To test the efficiency of the ship's air conditioning plant a visit was also paid to Elphinstone Inlet in the Persian Gulf, reputed to have the highest average temperature in the world, with the thermometer often reading 130 degrees F. [*January 1964*]

50

50 *Corunna runs on and on*

HMS Corunna was the first of the old Battle class destroyers to be converted and now re-commissioned for the second time as a Fleet Radar Picket – despite the changes in her silhouette, under her new face lay the body of a vessel that first emerged from Swan Hunter & Wigham Richardson's yard at Wallsend-on-Tyne in 1945.

In 1959 it was decided that four 'Later Battle' class destroyers, of which Corunna was the first, should be modernised to provide long-range air warning to the major units and in particular the NATO Strike Fleet. This necessitated the fitting of additional radio and radar equipment – the most striking result being the rotating bedstead aerial, plus the addition of the Seacat guided weapon system. [*March 1964*]

51 *'Can-do' Hartland's eastern cure-all*

HMS Hartland Point, the Far East Fleet's escort maintenance ship, boasted a bristling array of 40mm guns – more than any other ship in the Fleet. But her main armament was the "men who keep up the supply of steam, water and amps; men who strip down and service radar sets, mill brass sleeves, rebuild boats' stems, bend pipes, weld plates, make awnings, rewire directors and even bake bread rolls, pull out bad teeth and cure the 'dog' . . ."

She had begun life in Canada 20 years before when she was completed as a maintenance ship for landing ships. Too late to do her bit for the war effort, she lingered for years in Reserve until 1959, when she was modernised at Chatham and sent to the Far East where her motto 'Finis Coronat Opus' soon became translated from the elegant "The End Crowns the Work" to the abruptly expressive "Can Do" – her invariable reply to such varying demands as "Change a 4.5 inch barrel at the rush", "Send a hundred men to run armed boat patrols in Borneo" or "Entertain 1,600 under-privileged children on a banyan". [*May 1964*]

52 *Buccaneers in the South China Sea*

Two Buccaneers of HMS Victorious's 801 Sqn – the first fully operational squadron of this aircraft which was to see 30 years' service – are seen during exercises in the South China Sea. [*May 1964*]

51

52

53

53 *"Keep Cambrian at sea"*

The destroyer HMS Cambrian was back at the end of an 18 month general service commission that had seen plenty of action. It was just a week old – with the ship at sea for the first time operationally in 17 years since she had gone into reserve in 1946 – when the BBC reported her standing by HMS Pheasant in trouble off North Cornwall after her tow had parted in heavy seas.

After visiting Cardiff – her one and only UK "jolly" in the whole commission as it turned out – she was packed off East of Suez and was immediately absorbed into the complex web of South-East Asian politics, ordered to act as Gan guardship even before formally joining the Far East Fleet.

Having finally reached Singapore six weeks after sailing from the UK, Cambrian was soon out on exercises – and thus the pattern "keep Cambrian at sea" became firmly established. She was kept busy on the North Borneo patrol, pirate hunting in the Sulu Sea and ferrying Malaysian troops to Sarawak. A few days at Cebu in the Philippines made up her only period of relaxation in the Far East, after which she was despatched "on loan" to the Middle East Station – inevitably acting as Gan guardship again for a period on the way.

Christmas was spent in Aden Harbour in the tense atmosphere that followed the terrorist bombing that killed the Assistant British High Commissioner. Further south the rumblings of military unrest spread throughout East Africa. Cambrian was escorting the carrier Centaur from Aden to Singapore when Tanganyikan troops mutinied in their barracks at Dar-es-Salaam. Both ships diverted to the area – and it was Cambrian's 4.5 inch guns that poured a barrage of diversionary fire on waste ground within sight of the mutineers while 45 Commando landed from Centaur to sort them out – not HMS Rhyl's as Navy News along with the rest of the world's Press erroneously recorded.

From East Africa Cambrian made the long haul back across the Indian Ocean to take part in Exercise Jet 64 in the Bay of Bengal, after first spending a period in Singapore Dockyard to make good the ravages of three months' high-speed steaming in the Middle East. Soon she was on coastal patrol in East Malaya after reports of Indonesian activity on the Kelanatan coast. This was followed by a much-appreciated week in Hong Kong.

An eagerly awaited trip to Bangkok was cancelled owing to a minor mechanical defect which forced the ship to return to Singapore. Thence she was due to return home in company with HMS Diana – but out of the blue Cambrian found herself operating as Gan guardship for the third time. However an increased speed of passage and reduced shore time for the ship's company enabled her to reach Portsmouth on time having clocked up over 60,000 miles in 12 months. [*June 1964*]

54 *Changing face of the Rock*

The huge water catchment area has long been a familiar feature of this side of the Rock – but old timers who knew the quiet village at Catalan Bay would scarcely have recognised it by this time. A large modern hotel, a foretaste of further developments, rises from the sea at its foot. HMS Dreadnought in the foreground. [*December 1964*]

54

55

55 Mighty Albion's new role

HMS Albion again One of the first pictures taken after a long refit (the first since she was converted as a commando carrier) shows her undergoing full power trials and work-up before leaving for service in the Far East. The Wessex Mark 5s of 848 Naval Air Commando Squadron embarked in her had a better troop carrying capability than earlier naval helicopters. [*February 1965*]

56 Puma on the prowl around 33 ports

The Leopard Class frigate HMS Puma – seen here bows under during an exercise when the weather could have been kinder – was due to visit 33 ports in the course of a summer "Meet the Royal Navy" cruise attended by a lorry-borne exhibition. It was the kind of public relations/recruiting drive in which the Navy excelled in those days, affording opportunities for hundreds of Sea Cadets and members of school Combined Cadet Forces to spend time at sea. Today's much smaller Fleet no longer has the resources to spare from its tight programme of training and operations. [*March 1965*]

56

57 *Foxy lady takes flight*

A Sea Vixen is catapulted from HMS Centaur off Gibraltar as the planeguard helicopter maintains station. Visits to Naples, Istanbul and Izmir followed – during which, as ever, the ship's company entertained hundreds of orphans and other under-privileged local children to "pirate parties" on board, a practice that has endeared British sailors to generations of infants the world over. [*July 1965*]

57

58

60

58 *Royal Maidstone's main men*

The Queen talks to senior ratings of the Third Submarine Squadron on board the depot ship HMS Maidstone during a Review of the Fleet in the Clyde.

The Royal barge also drew alongside the nuclear-powered Fleet submarine HMS Dreadnought – to meet her first commanding officer, Cdr, later Admiral of the Fleet Lord Fieldhouse of Gosport, who would become the first submariner to be appointed Chief of the Defence Staff. [*September 1965*]

59 *Drawing for 'Drafty'*

'CND' banging square pegs into round holes does not refer to the Campaign for Nuclear Disarmament...

Charles Miles' first cartoon for Navy News in 1966 – he has produced a couple of thousand since – reflected the still enduring suspicion that Captain Naval Drafting's organisation was dedicated to posting 'Jack' to the one place he does not want to be.

59

Many of the sailor's difficulties would be resolved, said the accompanying article, "by more careful and frequent use of Drafting Preference Cards" – an oft-repeated refrain in Drafty's Column over the years, which 'Smiles' continues to illustrate with his customary cynicism.

60 *Wet and warm*

HMS Astute enters Aden on her way home to Plymouth. Part of the Devonport-based Second Submarine Squadron, she had been detached to exercise with ships of the Middle East Station and the Indian Navy, which had her operating out of Madras and Vishakhapatnam. On arrival in the Persian Gulf, where the water temperature hovered around 95 degrees, the submarine's divers removed her after hydroplanes for repair – a job normally carried out in dry dock – which earned them high praise for their "initiative, skill and resourcefulness" from the Flag Officer Submarines. Mr J P Mallalieu, the Defence Permanent Under Secretary, visited her during his tour of the Bahrein base – and was at Plymouth to welcome her home after a six month, 20,000 mile voyage that underlined her ability to operate for long periods away from a depot ship. [*January 1966*]

61

61 *Curtain call for support act*

HMS Adamant, seen here dressed overall at the Royal Review on the Clyde, was soon to go on the Disposal List. Known to nearly all submariners of the Second World War and since, she was completed in 1942 and was over 100 ft longer than her two sister depot ships Maidstone and Forth.

Two months after commissioning, she had sailed for the East, where she was intended to replace HMS Lucia and her river-boat stand-in, the Wu Chang, in Ceylon – but Admiral Somerville needed float repair facilities at Kilindisi in East Africa and directed her there instead.

Later in the year HMS Hekla became available and Adamant was released and sailed for Ceylon. Hekla, however, was sunk on passage by a German submarine. Adamant returned to East Africa. Later she sailed once more for Ceylon to become the depot ship of the Fourth Submarine Flotilla at Trincomalee – under the command of Captain "Tinsides" Ionides. She stayed there until April 1945, submarines of her flotilla having accounted for 255 Japanese vessels – when she moved to Freemantle for a few months before going on to Singapore and Hong Kong.

In 1948 she steamed home to join the Reserve Fleet until in 1953 a refit brought her into service again as depot ship of the Third Submarine Squadron at Rothesay and Faslane. In 1962 she sailed for Plymouth to support the Second Submarine Squadron – where she remained thereafter, occasionally taking her submarines off to the USA, Gibraltar and various British and European ports. [*March 1966*]

62

62 *Star ship was Pompey's enterprise*

Watched by the Portsmouth Dockyard men who built her, the Leander Class frigate HMS Sirius leaves harbour under her own power for the first time. Unlike their commercial counterparts, Royal Dockyards expected the Navy to commission, man and steam dockyard-built ships on Sea Trials. Here the ship's trials crew are neatly fallen in while, secretly in the waist, the dockyard men assemble, proud of their efforts.

Sirius's World War II cruiser predecessor had been built on the same slip and had maintained a close liaison with Portsmouth Football Club – it had already been decided that the new ship's sporting colours would be blue and white and she bore the same motto, "Heavens Light Our Guide" as the City of Portsmouth, sealing a link with the place of her birth that would be maintained for a quarter of a century. [*April 1966*]

63 Confrontation collection

Eighteen Wessex 5 helicopters of 848 Naval Air Squadron fly over HMS Albion at anchor off Labuan. Though talk of settlement and peace was in the air, the way of life for 16,000 officers and men of Britain's Far East Fleet was still dominated by one word – confrontation. Royal Navy helicopters had taken part in a huge movement of troops when they lifted three military units in Malaysian Borneo.

Operating from the commando ship, the Wessex heavy lift aircraft flew in men of 40 Cdo, RM, who replaced a Malaysian battalion in the Simangcang area of Sarawak's Second Division. Then they lifted the Malaysians into the Lundu District of the First Division, bringing out men of 42 Cdo who had completed a five month tour of Sarawak – their fifth in Borneo since their first arrival in December 1964 as part of the force which quelled the Brunei revolt.

Here for the first time in six months all the Wessex helicopters of 848 Squadron were embarked together after assisting the Security Forces against the Indonesian infiltrations. [*June 1966*]

63

64 All-British at Barrow

The first all-British nuclear Fleet submarine HMS Valiant commissions at Barrow-in-Furness. Valiant was similar in design to HMS Dreadnought, which had a US-built reactor, and cost £25m. Slightly larger, she boasted a then unusually spacious interior with two messes for ratings, six showers and a laundry. With a speed of over 30 knots, she was armed with homing torpedoes and had a crew of 12 officers and 90 ratings. [*August 1966*]

65 Still room for rum

Working up at Portland was the new Royal Fleet Auxiliary Lyness, first of the three new Fleet Supply ships – the others were Stromness and Tarbatness. Seen from the first as a store around which a ship could be built, her role was to replenish fleet units, ranging from carriers to minesweepers, with naval and victualling stores, rapidly and in large quantities while under way. She could carry around 100,000 different items – from bath plugs and curtain rods to aircraft wings and tyres. Eggs – 18,000 dozen of them – could be stored in a special compartment kept at freezing point. Together with 70 tons of meat and fish, 200 tons of groceries and 170 tons of vegetables, there was still room for 5,000 gallons of rum ... [*April 1967*]

65

66, 67

68

66, 67 **Advertising Hermes**

As HMS Hermes steamed through the submerged extinct volcanic crater of Santorin in the southern Aegean after a visit to Athens, an advertisement at the foot of the cliff-hanging town of Thira was seen to proclaim 'Hermes en Grece'. The carrier – under the command of Captain, later Admiral of the Fleet Lord Lewin – was shortly to pass through the Suez Canal to begin several months' service in the Far East. [*June 1967*]

68 **Last of the Lochs**

After completing more than 23 years' service, the last five continuously in the Far East, HMS Loch Fada, last of the Loch Class in the Navy, was on her way home from Singapore to pay off for disposal. Apart from four years in reserve in the mid-Fifties, she had been on continuous service on the Home, Middle East and Far East stations since the war, and on arrival at Portsmouth would have steamed nearly half a million miles – or more than 19 times around the world. [*September 1967*]

69 *Winning shot for Heron "phot"*

'Rockets Away' – a dramatic study of a Royal Navy Sea Vixen showing off her firepower – won Leading Airman Lowe of HMS Heron first prize in Class 3 (RN Aircraft) of the Peregrine Trophy competition – a showcase of the work of the RN photographic branch that Navy News features to this day. In the final judging, it also secured the top overall award. [*February 1968*]

69

70

70 *Demise of China Fleet*

As HMS Maryton, one of the Sixth Mine Countermeasures Squadron, arrived in the United Kingdom, HMS Fiskerton – seen here leaving Hong Kong after nine years' active duty in the Far East – was on her way home, and Woolaston and Wilkieston were due to leave the station soon.

The 8th MCM Squadron at Hong Kong was no more – they were the last true representatives of the China Fleet. In future, ships of the 6th MCM Squadron from Singapore would instead spend short periods of detached duty in and around the Crown Colony. [*February 1968*]

71 *Revenge – tenth of a proud name*

The launch of HMS Revenge, fourth and last of the Royal Navy's Polaris submarines. In common with the three other giant nuclear-powered submarines that would take over the role of providing the UK's strategic deterrent from the RAF's Vulcan bombers – Repulse, Renown and Resolution – Revenge would have two commanding officers and two crews, 'Port' and 'Starboard'.

Each had the benefit of unlimited fresh water for showers, cooking and fully-equipped laundry for a ship's company of 143 officers and men. With the completion of Revenge, the Polaris force, based at Faslane on the Clyde as the 10th Submarine Squadron, would become fully operational by 1970. This latest Revenge was the tenth in the Royal Navy to bear the name. The first was launched at Deptford in 1577, carried Sir Francis Drake during the fight against the Spanish Armada and was sunk after Sir Richard Grenville's epic battle off the Azores in 1591. The ninth Revenge was a battleship armed with eight 15 inch guns which joined the Grand Fleet in 1916, fought at the Battle of Jutland, and survived to 1948. [*April 1968*]

71

73

73 *Cooking with gas*

HMS Exmouth – the world's first major warship to be propelled by gas turbine engines – leaves Chatham for sea trials. She had a Rolls Royce Olympus engine for full power and two Rolls-Royce Proteus engines for cruising – both 'marinised' versions of well-proved and reliable engines used in a variety of commercial operations.

"The Royal Navy, which has pioneered the use of gas turbines in warships for over 20 years, intends using combinations of gas turbine machinery modules for all future major warships." [*July 1968*]

74 *Boom goes for bust*

After 43 years in commission, the Navy's Boom Defence School and premier Boom Defence Depot was paying off as a naval establishment.

On May 15 1925 a Boom Defence Training School was formed at Rosyth to teach the skills learned during 1914–18. It was commissioned eight months after the outbreak of the Second World War as HMS Rooke – now the parent establishment at Gibraltar.

HMS Rooke played an important part in the Navy's war effort and the security which the boom defences gave to our harbours gave many ship's crews cause for gratitude. It carried out a number of bizarre trials such as the 'Swiss Roll', a flexible floating causeway of wood and canvas designed to carry vehicles.

On July 1 1946 HMS Rooke was renamed HMS Safeguard to allow the name to be used for the naval base at Gibraltar.

With the decline of importance attached to boom defences, Safeguard's role gradually changed – until she became the 'Pooh Bah' of the Scotland Command, the establishment which handled everything nobody else could take on. It became a base for the Explosive Ordnance Disposal Team, for naval diving training and for seamanship and leadership training – functions which would continue at HMS Cochrane.

● HMS Barbican, a 'Bar' Class boom defence vessel, lays nets in the Firth of Forth during Admiral's Inspection. [*December 1968*]

72

72 *Old Colonial, newly independent*

When Mauritius became independent in March, 1968, it had been a British colony since it was ceded to Britain under the Treaty of Paris in 1814. The Royal Navy had had a presence there from 1962, when the wireless station was commissioned as HMS Mauritius. It remained an important part of the Navy's world-wide communications system. The main centre at Vacoas included excellent married quarters, schools and a beach club with chalets for week-end breaks. Here the Royal Navy enjoyed a thriving sporting life, with its own swimming pool and facilities for skin diving, shooting, and archery as well as rugby, football, tennis and squash, the tropical surroundings enhanced by the unmistakable atmosphere of old Colonial France. [*April 1968*]

74

75 Rough passage for the Press

When 400 sailors ride a fleet of little minesweepers head on into a Force ten at 12 knots, the result is ... 400 sick sailors. Well, a good many of them, anyway. When Daily Express reporter Jack Taylor accompanied nine Ton Class sweepers and the minelayer Abdiel on a run across the North Sea from HMS Lochinvar at Port Edgar on the Forth to Hamburg he was honest enough to admit to a severe attack of mal de mer during the worst passage most of the sailors could remember.

Yet on board the Chilcompton, another "landlubber newspaperman" was one of the few not to succumb to the elements, which downed the cook and most of the crew. Her CO, Lt Jeremy Sanders, cheerfully prepared dinner for his officers – "a meal cooked in conditions more suited to a rodeo cowboy than a chef."

They were determined to honour an appointment with the civic dignitaries of the ancient Hanseatic port. Many of them arrived when a cocktail party in HMS Abdiel was already under way – and few of them were in a state to enjoy the robust German hospitality. On another ship, HMS Belton, only two men had held on to the contents of their stomachs – the CO, Lt.-Cdr Tony Wilks, and the Ministry of Defence Press Officer, Jim Gray, who upheld the honour of his Navy News colleagues. We were made of stern stuff in those days ...

HMS Lewiston is the one getting a buffeting here. [*January 1969*]

75

76 From tiny acorns

A new technique of in-flight refuelling from a small ship – in this case, HMS Rothesay – enabled a big Wessex Mk 3 helicopter to stay on patrol for longer periods away from its parent vessel. [*February 1969*]

76

77, 78 **Beagle a natural selection**

HMS Beagle came under the spotlight as the 160th 'Ship of the Royal Navy'. First commissioned in the preceding year, she was the second of the Fawn Class of coastal survey vessels – and took the name of the Navy's most famous survey ship, the brig in which Charles Darwin made his historic voyage in 1831 – which was, in fact, the third HMS Beagle.

The term 'coastal' indicated the ability of this class to work inshore. Actually Beagle and her sisters Bulldog, Fawn and Fox were well able to undertake long ocean passages, operating in two-year periods between refits, in pairs for up to ten months without base support. Air-conditioned throughout, they were well suited for hydrographic research anywhere in the world. The 990 ton Beagle had a complement of only 38 officers and men and was not normally armed – though she could mount a 20mm gun at the after end of each bridge wing and had a small magazine in the fo'c'sle. In areas of unrest abroad, where the Foreign Office was particularly sensitive to the need to balance low-profile diplomacy against subtle pressure, her white-and-cream livery was less obviously threatening then the usual battleship grey. [*March 1969*]

● John Chancellor's study in oils depicts Darwin's Beagle in the Galapagos.

77

78

79, 80 **Fire at Valparaiso**

A 21 gun national salute to Peru is fired from the destroyer HMS Hampshire as she enters the breakwater at Callao. Together with the Leander Class frigates Arethusa and Juno, submarines Otus and Narwhal, supported by the fleet tanker Olwen and stores ship Lyness, she was making a goodwill cruise to five South American countries. The "chance of a lifetime" voyage was not without its moments of drama – while berthed at Valparaiso she helped extinguish a serious fire among bales of cotton on the dockside. They had the blaze well under control before the civilian fire brigade arrived.

● Sailors on board HMS Arethusa watch as HMS Juno moves into the same lock at Gatun while on passage through the Panama Canal. [*April 1969*]

79

80

81

81 *Confrontational cabaret – rice wine and skulls*

For the first time since the end of the Confrontation with Indonesia, the Royal Navy returned to Kuching, Sarawak. HM Ships Wilkieston (seen here) and Sheraton arrived to host the Commander Far East Fleet (Vice Admiral W D O'Brien) who was making an official visit to Malaysian Borneo. Sailors set out to visit a Dayak longhouse, where they were entertained by the Pengula (headman) with rice wine and a cabaret of traditional dances. "Among the most interesting but gruesome sights in the longhouse were the skulls still kept there from head-hunting days. We were assured that this custom had now ceased, although there were still lots of fearful-looking parangs hanging on the walls..." [*May 1969*]

82 *Old Bar ships it green*

With the transfer of the Boom Defence Depot at Loyang to the Singapore Government, HMS Barbain, the last RN unit there, travelled with it. The 28-year-old ship was towed out to the Far East in 1946 and remained there ever since. Strangely, she completed a third of her total steaming in the past six months – a cool "or not so cool" 9,180 miles. It had been quite a change from her normal duties – the laying, inspecting and renewing of the heavy moorings attached to the ships of the Far East Fleet in the roads off Singapore Naval Base. She had taken off across the Indian Ocean to Gan, stopping at Penang for fuel and water, riding into the teeth of the south-west monsoon. As the small ship (750 tons standard) pitched into the heavy swells, her captain estimated that she was scooping up through the 'horns' around five tons of water, which swirled down her decks often eight inches deep before pouring astern. At Gan she had to hold the fuel hulk Wave Victor – all 23,000 tons of her – while she was detached, by cutting through the cable, from her moorings. Trouble later struck when her main bearings had to be lowered. With no dockyard assistance, the ship's engine room staff set to, the RAF lent some ten-ton jacks and the repairs were completed in less than a fortnight. Making port at Masira off the South Arabian coast by way of Bombay did not mean any rest for her crew as they began a programme of renewing moorings for tankers supplying fuel to the RAF station there. No shore leave was given, the hands turned to at 0530 and secure was seldom before 2000.

On to Bahrain for major renewal jobs of moorings severely damaged by salt water corrosion. The return trip via Cochin took Barbain back into the monsoon, now blowing from nor'east, and the ship also caught the side effects of two cyclonic disturbances. "For 24 hours the ship rolled about 25 degrees either way – again it was about five tons per wave..."

"That passage of 1,980 miles in ten days must be about the longest ever for a 'Bar' vessel – not bad for a 28-year-old ship, and we certainly learnt something about what a 'Bar' can do." [*June 1969*]

82

83 *Fine sieve for Wasp stingers*

Into the attack goes a Royal Navy Wasp helicopter, loosing off an AS 12 missile. The Wasp, designed purely as an extension of the small ship's anti-submarine armoury, was well-suited to carry this French-designed weapon in a stand-off attack against a small, fast-moving surface target such as the newly appearing fast missile-carrying patrol boats.

"The weapon is very simple and reliable, but its accuracy depends entirely on the skill of its aimer. The aimer literally drives the missile onto the target by means of a control stick mounted in the helicopter which remotely controls the missile in the same way as the pilot flies the aircraft.

"Such a task requires a great deal of co-ordination and the ability to react quickly to changes of situation; indeed, because of the job's complexity, selection is through a very fine sieve and only the elite join the ranks of AS 12 missile aimers." [*November 1969*]

83

84 *Ivan eyes Eagle*

HMS Eagle was the focus of attention of Russian ships during the NATO exercise Deep Furrow in the Mediterranean. Here a Soviet Petya Class takes a close look, showing particular interest in flying operations. [*December 1969*]

84

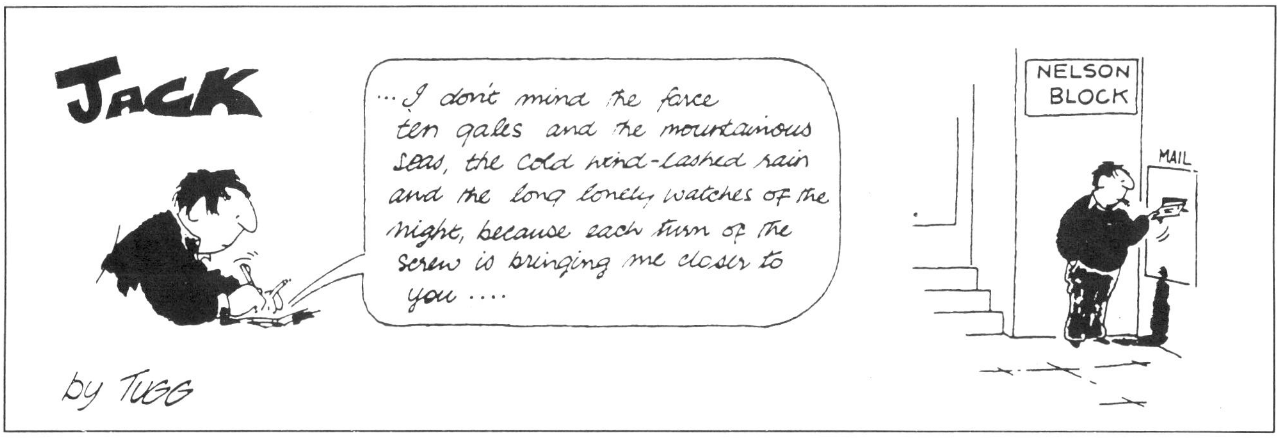

JACK
... I don't mind the force ten gales and the mountainous seas, the cold wind-lashed rain and the long lonely watches of the night, because each turn of the screw is bringing me closer to you ....
NELSON BLOCK
MAIL
by TUGG

85 *Thunderbirds are go!*

Lady Penelope (London model Penny Snow) met two sailors from HMS Penelope when FAB 1, the £11,000 car – well, it was a lot of money for a motor then – used to promote the hit "Thunderbirds" TV puppet show visited a Plymouth garage. "Thunderbirds" was the latest in a series of hugely successful wired-up space age vehicles for marionettes that would enjoy a revival over 20 years later.

The lucky lads supporting Lady P – no strings attached – are OS Allan Owen (right) and OEM David Phelps. [*February 1970*]

85

86 *Mod gear for snowmen*

45 Royal Marines Commando was the first specialised unit to be fully equipped and trained for mountain and Arctic warfare and would be stationed at RN air station Arbroath with the departure of the Fleet Air Arm early in 1971. The Marines would be trained to survive and fight in temperatures often as low as minus 40 degrees Centigrade – and were already in Norway, putting in three months vigorous practice for their role as part of the UK's commitment to the defence of NATO's northern flank. [*February 1970*]

86

87

88

87, 88 *Dad's Army tank's day out*

A tank rumbling over the causeway from Whale Island at Portsmouth in the early days of World War II must have heartened the civilian population – well, maybe ... After Dunkirk, invasion was hourly expected and there was a desperate resort to any sort of weapon of defence.

Such a one, in the proud tradition of 'Dad's Army', was a 'land ship' of 1914-18 vintage, presented to the gunnery school at HMS Excellent by the Army – who, in 1916, finding that their gunners were unused to firing from a moving, pitching platform, wisely concluded that seamen would make the best tutors and transferred 136 officers and 2,413 men to Whale Island, whence they were embarked in MTBs to learn their skill.

Over twenty years later, with the invasion scare of 1940 at its height, Second Lieutenant A Menhenick of the Royal Army Service Corps pondered the possibilities of the old tank – and the Captain of Excellent gave his permission to see what could be done with it. No spares were available, but another tank on Southsea front was stripped to repair the deficiencies – and after a month spent spraying the tracks with a mixture of paraffin and oil, Menhenick started the huge engine and gingerly drove it off its plinth.

He and his Corporal took off for a trial run – proudly flying a large White Ensign from the stern – and got as far as the Traveller's Rest in Somers Road, where, hot, exhausted and covered in oil they poured 40 pints of water into their charge – and several pints of ale into themselves – before beginning the return trip to 'Whaley'.

With the field of vision limited by the giant tracks, and both of them deafened by the shattering noise inside, they thundered along until Menhenick suddenly spotted a policeman frantically waving his arms in the middle of the road. Twenty-sevens tons of armour came to a grinding halt and the pair clambered out – to find, pinned under the tank's left sponson, the total wreck of a commercial traveller's car, which had been sliced in half as it stood parked somewhere en route ...

Fortunately the tank's intended new role was never tested – but after the passage of another 30 years CPO Ray Wield, an ordnance electrical artificer who was secretary of Whale Island's CPOs Mess, became the second man to be fired with enthusiasm to get the big beast moving again – and after three years' restoration work the Mk IV tank found a new home at the Tank Museum at Bovington. [*March 1970*]

89

89 Dance spectacular

Water, cloud and ships of the Western Fleet against a background of Gibraltar combine to make this panoramic seascape. The ships, pictured during manoeuvring exercises, are the aircraft carrier HMS Hermes, the destroyer HMS Decoy, and the Leander class frigates Ajax, Minerva, Charybdis and Danae. [*April 1970*]

90 Relaunching Yarnton risks grounding

"HMS Yarnton just launched? You must be joking!" But that is what did happen when the 14-year-old minesweeper completed a maintenance period at the Bahrain slipway. When work of this kind is completed, ships are not winched down into the water but are allowed to slide on a cradle."

For the first time in over 40 years two Royal Navy ships – Yarnton in company with HMS Puncheston – had made passage through the Clarence Strait between the coast of Iran and Qeshm Island.

The two minesweepers of the 9th Mine Counter Measures Squadron based on Bahrein had a tough time negotiating the 70 mile-long strait, which narrows to 14 miles, is filled with sandbanks and skirted for much of its length by mangrove swamps. Surveys were old and lacking in detail and the frequently shifting sandbanks made passage a hazardous and unpredictable operation. A small launch was sent ahead to sound with lead and line under the command of Yarnton's midshipman, who thus earned himself a permanent niche in the survey world.

There followed seven hours of painstaking navigation – and at one point the pilot, asked for his advice, hurriedly replied: 'Anchor – or better still turn back!'

In the final stretch, where the channel at times doubled back on itself, there was one nasty shock when the echo sounder gave a reading of $1^1/_2$ fathoms. [*May 1970*]

90

91 **Upton opens for business**

During a period of two months detached service from the 1st Mine Counter Measures Squadron based at Port Edgar, HMS Upton visited Ghent.

She also spent five days at Porthcawl, where she was officially 'adopted', swept live mines off the coast of Holland, visited Le Havre and operated for a week from Portsmouth and Portland.

As a result of the minesweeping programme, carried out with HMS Lewiston and ships of the Dutch, French, Belgian and German navies, an old minefield of 10,000 mines was cleared, and an extensive area reopened to merchant shipping for the first time since the Second World War. *[July 1970]*

91

92

92 *Swift sword in the Solent*

Slicing through the water as a Scimitar should, the Royal Navy's new fast training boat cuts a dash in the Solent a couple of days after being commissioned. The first of three ordered in January 1969 – Cutlass and Sabre were the others – she followed the Brave Class of Coastal Forces-type vessels built by Vosper Thornycroft a decade before. Powered by three Rolls-Royce Proteus gas turbines, with diesels for cruising and manoeuvring, she achieved speeds of up to 58 knots. [*August 1970*]

93

93 *Wessex 'bombs' Ennerdale*

The Governor of the Seychelles thanked the Royal Navy for breaking up the wreck of the RFA Ennerdale and sweeping away fears of large-scale oil pollution by pioneering a brand new demolition technique.

The 62,000 ton tanker, with oil trapped in her storage tanks, sank after striking submerged and uncharted coral seven miles from Port Victoria. Salvage was impossible and the wreck was broken up by a method developed by the Far East Fleet of 'bombing' from a helicopter.

The technique involved placing demolition charges – anti-submarine mortar bombs and torpedo warheads – lowered from a Wessex helicopter. Because of strong currents it was too dangerous to use divers to set them in position. The fuses were activated from the helicopter and a two-minute time delay gave the aircraft time to get clear. [*October 1970*]

94

94 Rum question, by Jove

"Was Jupiter's the last tot?"

The Leander Class frigate, then operating in the West Indies, claimed the distinction – "We were furthest west and working tropical routine when the sad day occurred," she reported.

The Jupiter, showing the flag with HMS Sirius, celebrated her first birthday off Andros Island, having steamed 24,000 miles in 1,800 hours. She was the first Jupiter in these waters since 1782, when Admiral Rodney hoisted his flag in Jamaica.

Life had been far from dull since her arrival on station in April, with visits to Grand Bahama, Key West, Puerto Rico, Anguilla, Antigua, St Vincent, St Lucia, St Thomas, Barbados – and Trinidad, where she stood by during riots. [*November 1970*]

95 Endurance meets up with Chay Blyth

The ice patrol ship HMS Endurance made a rendezvous with round-the world yachtsman Chay Blyth 80 miles east of Cape Horn – and found the 'British Steel' rocking gently on a calm sea.

In the summer of this year former paratrooper Chay received a warm welcome from HMS Ark Royal as he neared the end of the first solo, nonstop voyage round the globe by the east-west route. His 17 ton yacht was spotted by the carrier in the Atlantic when she was 500 miles from landfall at Hamble, Hants [*February 1971*]

95

96 Frigate saves disabled Finn

For 42 anxious hours, with HMS Ashanti alongside, a naval party worked aboard the huge Finnish tanker Pegny, disabled in the Persian Gulf, to restore power before she drifted out of deep water.

Two of the 96,000 ton vessel's generators had burnt out – and though the third was serviceable, being driven by steam it could not be started without the ship having power of her own.

Initially, an advance party was flown to the tanker in Ashanti's Wasp helicopter and winched down. On a second sortie the pilot decided there was ample space to land on her vast deck.

In spite of a strong wind, the sea was calm and the Ashanti was able to move in close. It was an anxious time as the two ships were drifting to an area where the Pegny, drawing 48 feet, would almost certainly have grounded – and when power was restored there was barely a mile to go. The frigate's efforts, said the tanker's Master later, had "certainly saved the ship". [*March 1971*]

97 Prized portfolio

"Some of the finest pictures of a warship in heavy seas ever offered", said the Editor of the Photographic Year Book on receiving a portfolio from NA Roger Ball, then on the staff of the Commander-in-Chief Western Fleet. For this shot of HMS Andromeda, Ball used his own Mamiya C350 with an 80mm lens. [*April 1971*]

96

97

99

98

98 *The one that winged Nelson*

The old Spanish cannon aimed at HMS Blake across the harbour at Santa Cruz, Tenerife once took a heavy toll among English sailors, but it was a long time since 'El Tigre' last fired a shot in anger. Local legend – recorded on a brass plaque fixed to its side – claims that it delivered the grape-shot which shattered Nelson's right arm when he attempted to capture Santa Cruz in 1797.

99 *Any which way for Warspite*

HMS Warspite – the second all-British nuclear-powered submarine – was set up for a mock booking after she claimed to be the first ship of the Royal Navy to manage to navigate without a magnetic compass, using gyro compass only.

Traffic wardens were waiting on the jetty at Portsmouth when she arrived for a short visit – her first appearance in a UK port apart from her base at Faslane – before going on to Chatham for a long refit.

And Third Officer Rose Locke, a member of the staff of the 1st Submarine Squadron across the water at Gosport, presented her commanding officer Cdr Christopher Wood with a motorist's magnetic compass – "just in case". [*July 1971*]

100 *The huntress hangs on to Haslar Creek*

On a calm summer's evening HM Submarine Artemis – at 24 one of the Navy's oldest warships in commission – sank in about 30 ft of water at her moorings alongside the jetty at HMS Dolphin, Gosport.

Down with her, to spend the next ten hours in a forward torpedo stowage compartment until escaping to safety, went three ratings.

Although they could have been got out at any time, attempts were made during the night to lift the 1,120 ton boat from the clinging mud of Haslar Creek, the dramatic scene watched by many submariners and newsmen under the glare of arc lights.

Finally the decision was made to use the escape hatch and one by one the trapped men came to the surface soon after five o'clock in the morning.

Here the submarine is seen sometime later, starting to refloat. [*August 1971*]

101

101 D-Day for Belfast

Against London's skyscraper backcloth HMS Belfast forms a picture of naval might as she is drawn into position at her final mooring just above Tower Bridge.

The largest cruiser ever built for the Royal Navy, veteran of the Battle of North Cape in which she shared in the destruction of the Scharnhorst, she now became one of the capital's major tourist attractions as the last remaining example of a big-gun cruiser. She remains also the last major warship to have taken part in D-Day. [*November 1971*]

102 Badger baiting Royal Knight

Not for the first time, the Russians had been displaying a close interest in the activities of HMS Ark Royal. This time her attendant was a Badger – the NATO code name for the Tupolev bomber TU-16. The Ark was taking part in Exercise Royal Knight in the Norwegian Sea, operating as part of the NATO Strike Fleet with other British and American, German, Dutch and Norwegian ships.

102

103 Trouser suit – and no tiara

Princess Anne on board HMS Renown with the Polaris submarine's commanding officer Cdr Tony Pogson and members of her crew. During a visit to the Clyde Submarine Base the Princess opened a new extension to the Drumfork Club on the Churchill married quarter estate. For her day-time engagements she wore a chocolate brown trouser suit – and her appearance disappointed one little girl from the club's playgroup: "I thought all princesses wore bands in their hair," she said. The Princess laughingly responded: "I'm sorry, but I can't do anything about it – I can't wear tiaras all the time!"

104 Beaten to it at Bengal

The carrier HMS Albion steams off at a rumbling 24 knots towards the Bay of Bengal to assist with the evacuation of civilians from East Pakistan during the country's two-week war with India. Here she is refuelling from the RFA Tideflow – with a large Union Jack painted on her flight deck to avoid any unfortunate mistakes in identification. In the event the British personnel were taken off by the RAF and the Albion altered course to spend five days at Gan. [*February 1972*]

103

104

105

106

105 **Breaking ice records**

After nine weeks away from base at HMS Daedalus a 50 ton hovercraft operated by the British Interservice Hovercraft unit returned home following completion of cold weather trials in the Baltic.

The first BH7 built by the British Hovercraft Corporation had completed the 1,100 mile journey to its operating base at Galo, Sweden under its own power at an overall speed in excess of 30 knots. Commanded by Cdr Peter Reynolds and with a crew of 28 sailors, soldiers and airmen, the craft established a number of unofficial records – including the longest open-sea journey completed by a hovercraft – and sustained speeds of over 55 knots in the Baltic. Top speed recorded was 74 knots over ice.

During the over-ice trials the BH7 penetrated deep into the Gulf of Bothnia, encountering ice ridges 3-4ft high. [*May 1972*]

106 **Fire and fog off Durban**

HMS Lowestoft fought fire, fog and rising seas to save a crippled tanker which had drifted within half-a-mile of going aground and causing large-scale pollution on South African shores.

The frigate was steaming from Simonstown to Durban when Port Elizabeth Radio warned that the Liberian SS Silver Castle, which had been in collision the previous day, was on fire with members of her crew missing.

Arriving on the scene, the Lowestoft found the tanker's entire after part ravaged by fire, with oil leaking from a large hole in the port side.

Her hoses brought the blaze under control and a tow was quickly passed – but the laden tanker, listing to port with her rudder jammed, proved very difficult to control. The tow had to be slipped and repassed in the dark before headway could be made to seaward. Besides securing the tow and fighting the fires, the boarding party was also struggling to move the rudder. A fire in the compartment below made the heat and smoke intense in the tiller flat, but eventually the rudder was disconnected from the burned-out engine and controlled with tackles. Then a dense fog rolled in and for two hours the tanker was invisible. When the fog lifted, the wind and sea rose and the tow parted. A new tow was passed – and then a salvage tug arrived to relieve the Lowestoft of her burden, allowing her to resume her interrupted passage. [*June 1972*]

107 **Ghostly chink in the gunbay**

What sadder sight could any gunnery officer witness than the removal of his beloved 4.5 inch turret? HMS Penelope's guns had been cocooned since 1966, but at least their presence had offered quiet encouragement... Now, after a delicate operation at Devonport, all that remained of them was a big hole in the deck.

Around 700 rounds per barrel were fired before the Penelope had begun duty as a scientific trials ship – and there were still those aboard who could remember when the cry "Four-point-five engage!" had echoed around the passageways. Now the only sound heard would be the chink of wine bottles coming up the shell hoists – the vacant gunbay was to become a wardroom annexe to house extra scientific staff. [*July 1972*]

107

108 Moment the mortar fired

Lucky shot – the cameraman manages to freeze the missile at the right moment as HMS Rothesay tests her mortars during a visit to Fremantle in Western Australia. [*August 1972*]

109 Kelly's Eye

Eighteen-year-old Wren Writer Lesley Talbot – the only girl in HMS Sultan's Volunteer Band – catches the eye of Admiral of the Fleet Earl Mountbatten of Burma, visiting HMS Mercury.

He was at the Royal Navy Signals School at Petersfield, Hants to formally name the new entry squadron there for his famous wartime destroyer command HMS Kelly, immortalised in the film "In Which We Serve". [*August 1972*]

110 Ikara calls for quick reaction

Ikara, the Australian anti-submarine missile, was fired from a Leander Class frigate for the first time when successful tests were held off Plymouth from the lead ship of the class.

HMS Leander started her sea trials by testing the weapon's launcher which, with associated handling rooms and magazine, had replaced the 4.5 inch gun system. Leander had also been fitted with a computerised operations room – the Ferranti computer was a vital part of the action process, enabling the command to reduce reaction time to any threat to a minimum. The whole system, together with the Wasp helicopter, made her the most advanced anti-submarine frigate then in service in the Fleet. [*March 1973*]

109

110

111

111 'Warship' short on glamour

When the first part of what was to be the highly successful BBC drama series 'Warship' was transmitted, HMS Phoebe, doubling as 'HMS Hero' was busy filming at Devonport with the armament vessel Throsk and would go on to Portland to make another two episodes.

The 'Warship' theme had been recorded by the Royal Marines Band and released as a single and LP with a picture of Phoebe on the cover. In July Lieut. Cdr Ian MacKintosh's novel would appear.

"I hope that our viewers will forgive the fact that, as many of the episodes take place entirely at sea, the series cannot boast an abundance of ladies," – the author apologised. "But there is an extremely pretty girl in episode four, and I hope the Navy will accept that I did my best for them in that quarter." [*June 1973*]

112 Tenacious little fighter

The latest Vosper small-combatant creation, the Tenacity, bought by the Royal Navy for the Fisheries Protection Squadron. With a Proteus installation, these 144 foot craft had a speed of 38 knots and a selection of armament schemes, including anti-shipping missiles such as Exocet, and modern fast-firing guns. [*September 1973*]

112

113 *New look for Rooke*

New accommodation blocks and the newly-erected 89 ft mast can be seen in this view of the HMS Rooke foreshore from Coaling Island. The new look for the RN establishment at Gibraltar was nearing completion at last, replacing the conglomeration of utility buildings more familiar to visitors in the post-war era [*October 1973*]

114 *Wartime soul of Dover*

HMS Lynx steams past the white cliffs of Dover during a 'Meet the Navy' visit to the busy cross-Channel port – where an RN shore base of the same name was once located.

HMS Lynx was the World War II anti submarine establishment at Dover, opened in 1939, which had its headquarters in an hotel, was damaged by bombing in 1941 and 1942 and finally closed in 1946. [*November 1973*]

113

114

115

117

115 **Theory into practice**

Only two days after HMS Hampshire's 'board and tow' exercise with RFA Olwen had been cancelled by Force 10 winds off Portland, a signal was intercepted from the Cypriot coaster Zodiac Steve, drifting with an engine room fire 17 miles off Portland Bill.

Swiftly despatched by the Flag Officer Sea Training to assist, the Hampshire was able to put her work-up plan to proper use. The Zodiac Steve's Chief Engineer, suffering from burns and shock, was taken by SAR helicopter to the destroyer for medical examination before being flown to Portland for further treatment – and once outside Portland Harbour the tow was taken over by Admiralty tugs. [*March 1974*]

116 **Britannia round the world in 185 days**

Conditions were lively for sailing and surfing when HMY Britannia and HMAS Torrens anchored off Norfolk Island.

Around the world in 185 days – the Royal Yacht had visited the Galapagos Islands, Tahiti, Fiji, New Zealand, Australia, Bali, Papua New Guinea, Singapore, Mauritius and Casablanca in the course of a cruise which saw members of the Royal Family in New Zealand for the Tenth British Commonwealth Games. The Prince of Wales, then serving in HMS Jupiter, joined the Royal party in Britannia for part of the tour, as did Admiral of the Fleet Earl Mountbatten.

After Norfolk Island – where some of the Bounty mutineers' descendants still live – the Britannia headed for the New Hebrides and after visiting Vila arrived off Pentecost Island to watch the famous land divers jump off a 70 ft tower.

Next came Santo and then the Solomon Islands. Honiara was here the scene of battles between the Japanese and American fleets in World War II – Ironbottom Sound was so named because of the number of warships sunk in the area.

116

At Port Moresby the yachtsmen watched a re-enactment of the sad end of missionary the Rev James Chalmers – murdered and subsequently eaten by the cannibal population of Goaribari Island in 1901.

The Queen flew to Australia for a 10-day tour – but was recalled to the UK after two days for the General Election. The Duke of Edinburgh and Earl Mountbatten joined the Britannia at Darwin and sailed to Bali, where The Queen rejoined the ship, final visits of the Royal tour being paid here and at Jakarta, the capital of Indonesia. When the Britannia arrived home at Portsmouth, she had been away six months and steamed 35,570 miles, visiting 18 countries. [*June 1974*]

117 **An end to confusion, Nelson confides**

The name of Nelson, missing from the Navy List since the battleship HMS Nelson was sold in 1948, was reinstated with due ceremony with the renaming of the Royal Naval Barracks, Portsmouth. So ended the anomaly of having an HMS Victory 'double' in Pompey – the name given to the barracks as well as to Nelson's famous flagship at Trafalgar.

In 1903 King Edward VII ordered that sailors from the RN Barracks should wear Victory cap tallies. The old wooden wall was slowly decaying at her moorings in the harbour and as the Navy had no plans to save her it seemed her name, too, would soon disappear. Public subscription saved her for the nation – and so began a period of confusion for both Service and public. Each summer holiday visitors presented themselves at the gates of the Barracks, at the nameboard 'HMS Victory', only to find they must trek to the other end of Queen Street to find the ship in her ancient dry dock in the Naval Base.

Many of the old sailors attending the renaming ceremony were surprised to see how much the barracks had changed – in its new incarnation most of the old red-brick buildings had been replaced by modern concrete and glass blocks, fulfilling the modern establishment's primary role as a fleet accommodation centre.

The magnificent bell of the previous HMS Nelson, returned to Newcastle's maritime and science museum after the battleship was broken up in 1949, was once more in commission. Originally presented by the people of Newcastle to commemorate the ship's building on the Tyne, it now had pride of place in the home of the Royal Navy – also the home of Navy News!

• The building overshadowing the ceremonials attended by the Commander-in-Chief Naval Home Command, Admiral Sir Derek Empson, is the Petty Officers' Mess. [*September 1974*]

118 **Chief waves goodbye**

For many years a familiar sight at Portland, the last of the Wave Class fleet tankers RFA Wave Chief left for Rosyth on her final voyage before going for disposal.

It was a particularly sad moment for her master, Captain David Campbell, who had first served in her as a cadet during the Korean War. The Wave Chief (8,200 tons standard displacement, 16,650 tons full load) was launched at Govan in 1946. [*October 1974*]

118

119

119 Ajax power makes a clean sweep

After doing duty as guardship during Cowes Week, HMS Ajax was off to Cyprus to relieve HMS Devonshire. She soon had urgent work to do – with HMS Rhyl she was detailed to take off 250 British passport holders, stranded after the Turkish invasion in the occupied port of Famagusta. This was achieved smoothly and the passengers were later off-loaded at Akrotiri to be flown home by the RAF. [*October 1974*]

120 Whiskey-Jack

Closely shadowed by the anti-submarine frigate HMS Rhyl, a Soviet Whiskey-class submarine passes through the Channel.

After playing a prominent part in the Cyprus evacuation, a number of cheques had been sent to the ship by grateful refugees. They were forwarded to the Royal National Lifeboat Institution at the request of the ship's company. [*December 1974*]

121 Anchors away

HMS Hampshire, "all lit up" in Grand Harbour, Malta, while acting as Commander-in-Chief's flagship. Later the guided missile destroyer sailed to join the carrier HMS Ark Royal for exercises in the central Mediterranean. The ship spent two stormy days anchored in the bay of Porto di Stefano near Maddalena in Sardinia – the bay where Nelson lost four of his ships when they dragged their anchors in a gale and ended up on the rocks.

The Hampshire did likewise – but fortunately escaped the fate of the hero of Trafalgar's consorts. [*January 1975*]

120

121

122

122 *Gazelle sprung from Bulwark*

First deck landings and take-offs of the new Gazelle helicopter from a Royal Navy ship took place from HMS Bulwark at Plymouth, when three aircraft from 3 Commando Brigade Air Squadron Royal Marines carried out landing trials on the commando carrier.

A single-engine five-seat helicopter with skid undercarriage, the Gazelle was a joint Anglo-French production by Westlands and Aerospatiale. [*April 1975*]

123 Ducklings minus their mother

HM ships Wolverton, Beachampton, Wasperton, Yarnton and Monkton, minus HMS Chichester, the colony's permanent guardship, in close formation to celebrate their award of the Wilkinson Peace Prize for the work of the Hong Kong Squadron in supporting the local community and its surrounding areas in the fight against illegal immigration and narcotics smugglers.

It went much further than that – well-suited for reaching isolated islands and areas of the colony not easily accessible other than by sea, the "ducklings" had given help to outlying villages where materials and ready labour were often unobtainable. Pipelines had been constructed, schoolrooms modernised, sports pitches laid out, generators fitted and piers and jetties repaired.

And with Hong Kong in the 'typhoon belt' there was the seasonal disaster risk in which the squadron was at hand to help if necessary – each vessel ranging twice a year for a month at a time farther afield to the Philippines, Thailand, Malaysia, Indonesia and Singapore. [*June 1975*]

123

124 Brazilian interlude for Blake

Fresh from her Far East deployment, the helicopter cruiser HMS Blake follows HMS Ark Royal into Rio harbour. The end of visits to South American ports by Royal Navy ships had their finale with an exercise with the Brazilians before the return home under the command of the Flag Officer First Flotilla, Vice-Admiral Henry Leach. [*July 1975*]

125 Sharks raise curtain at Culdrose

Making their first appearance at the RN air station Culdrose's International Air Day were the Sharks – the Gazelle helicopter display team of 705 Squadron based there.

The first of the Anglo-French turbine-powered trainers was delivered to Culdrose in the summer of 1973. With a cruising speed of over 150mph and a top speed of almost 200mph, the Gazelle was a good-looking, spectacular performer. [*August 1975*]

126 Highest honours enshrined

The Duke of Edinburgh meets relatives of ten Royal Marines who won the Victoria Cross as he arrives at Eastney, Portsmouth to open the Royal Marines Museum's new home in the Barracks old officers' mess.

124

CU
ROYAL NAVY 48
ROYAL NAVY 53
CU
ROYAL NAVY 45
CU
XW895 ROYAL NAVY 51
CU
XW863 ROYAL NAVY 42

125

126

127

127 **Space shot**

The Russian space satellite ships Vladimir Komarov and Yuri Gagarin provided HMS Argonaut's photographer with some unusual pictures when the Soviet ships met off the coast of Nova Scotia before operating together during the joint USA-USSR space shot.

With the fog descending off Sable Bank, the frigate's Wasp helicopter had to be launched at short notice while carrying out Canadian operations with the Standing Naval Force Atlantic between Halifax, Nova Scotia, and Newport, Rhode Island. [*September 1975*]

128

129

128 **Rigs receive rapid Reward**

Following anonymous bomb warnings to the police, newspapers and oil companies, HMS Reward was on the scene in two hours to provide headquarters and support for five RN divers who carried out a search of three gas production platforms in the North Sea.

Members of the Scotland and Northern Ireland Explosive Ordnance Disposal Team were flown in a Sea King helicopter of 819 Squadron from their base at Rosyth to platforms Arpett Alpha, Hewett Alpha and Arpett Bravo. [*October 1975*]

129 **Patience of Penelope**

HMS Penelope stands guard over all that remains visible of the Soviet fishing vessel Gorizont in the English Channel. The 4,500 ton Gorizont sank after a collision with a Moroccan cargo ship 25 miles off the Isle of Wight – but her bow, jutting 40ft out of the water, remained a hazard to shipping. HMS Penelope and HMS London were among the first on the scene. [*January 1976*]

130 Bound together off Belize

A joint-Service show of strength off the coast of Belize, as two RAF Harriers of No 1 Squadron based at Wittering fly over the Tribal Class frigate HMS Nubian. The Nubian was in the Caribbean in company with HMS Zulu, which had relieved HMS Minerva as the second West Indies Station frigate. [*January 1976*]

130

131 'Hands keep clear of the port side'

The 'Cod War' drags on... HMS Andromeda became closely involved with the Icelandic Coastguard gunboat Thor in the protracted dispute over fishery limits – too close for comfort, as these pictures show.

The Andromeda was protecting the trawler Ross Resolution at the time of the incident. This is how it was described from the bridge: '... Thor, finding herself held off by Andromeda, turned towards the trawler menacing both the trawler and Andromeda with a very dangerous potential collision situation. Fortunately Andromeda was able to go through the gap...

"Thor then turned to make a run at the trawler Portia and Andromeda once more turned into a defensive position. The events of the next few minutes are difficult to explain as it seems impossible that any seaman would purposely hazard his ship and crew by such actions in such a hostile environment. When it became apparent that Thor could not get at the trawler, she turned hard towards Andromeda from a parallel course without slackening her course.

"Despite full engine speed and rudder application, Andromeda was unable to avoid the inevitable collision and the starboard side of Thor's bow hit Andromeda's port quarter, demolishing guardrails and fittings."

In circumstances like these, small wonder the pipe "Hands keep clear of the port side" had become a familiar sound aboard RN frigates. [*February 1976*]

131

1 2 3 4

132

132 **Hermes in the frozen North**

45 Commando Royal Marines were embarked in the commando carrier HMS Hermes for Exercise Clockwork and a NATO Northern Region Exercise Atlas Express, together with a company of the Royal Netherlands Marine Corps, an Army artillery battery, a troop of Royal Engineers and a detachment of Royal Navy Wessex helicopters. Hermes is seen here at Narvik in mid January. [*February 1976*]

133

133 **Anchored to the deck**

"I've done my packing and I'm all ready to go – but how do I get the HMS Terror anchor home?"

That was the problem confronting Second Officer Ros Allchin, among the last of Royal Navy personnel to leave Singapore when she flew back to the UK in an RAF VC 10.

The anchor had been outside the wardroom at Terror since the Second World War. Now HMS Terror was to become Terror Camp for the Singapore Armed Forces, whose Midshipmen's School and School of Naval Training were already in residence. It is still there... [*March 1976*]

134 Through a Whiskey glass, darkly

Russian sailors cram the conning tower of a Whiskey-class submarine in the Straits of Dover – hoping for a sight of the Lieut. The Prince of Wales, commanding officer of HMS Bronington.

The minesweeper had been despatched at short notice to shadow the Soviet vessel, and kept her under close surveillance for two days after tracking her down – in appalling visibility – at the entrance to the Channel. [*June 1976*]

134

135 Key of the door at Daedalus

One of 781 Squadron's pair of 21-year-old Sea Devons on the runway at HMS Daedalus. Main function of the Squadron, based at the Lee-on-Solent naval air station since 1939, was to provide communication flights for VIPs, naval and other service personnel.

The aircraft celebrating their coming of age could be converted for use as flying ambulances. Other roles included providing targets for naval gunnery ranges near Portsmouth and patrol flights for fishery protection purposes. [*June 1976*]

135

136

136 San Juan and all that jazz

HMS Danae leaves San Juan, Puerto Rico. She had been in Roosevelt Roads for Exercise Springboard after a visit to New Orleans – the world centre of jazz – and was moving on to a weekend at Fort Lauderdale, Florida before joining in the multi-national Exercise Safe Pass in the western Atlantic. This ended in Halifax, Nova Scotia – where, competing against Canadian, German, Dutch and American ships, the frigate won a Standing Force Atlantic Olympiad.

Three weeks later the squadron crossed the Atlantic for Exercise Open Game off the north-west coast of Africa and in the Mediterranean. A three-day visit to Lisbon followed, before the Danae took her leave of her companions in the North Sea. During the deployment, she had steamed well over 30,000 miles. [*June 1976*]

137

138

137 *Revenge revived*

Navy News was tempted to caption this picture "A recent picture of HMS Revenge" – but that might have raised a few eyebrows among those who remembered that the battleship was scrapped in 1948...

The highly realistic portrait was actually prepared in a static water tank at RN air station Culdrose – with a radio-controlled 3ft hand-built model standing in for the genuine article.

With every detail impressively scaled down, the model had been started 41 years before by Mr Edward James Harding, who joined the Revenge as a boy seaman in 1913 and fought in the Battle of Jutland.

On retiring from the Royal Navy as a chief petty officer in 1935, he began a painstaking task which took him 12 years to complete. Mr Harding died in 1957 and the model lay high and dry for years, gathering dust in a variety of garages and lofts before his grandson, Mr Michael Harding, a former Fleet Air Arm mechanic later employed in maintaining helicopters at Culdrose, undertook the task of renovation. [*July 1976*]

138 *Lincoln addresses the Cod War – too late*

HMS Lincoln, completing an eight-day patrol of the North Sea oil rigs, displays her timber-reinforced bows – a 'Cod War' modification which was never put to the test as the dispute was settled before she could sail for Icelandic waters.

The rig in the picture is the Shell/Esso 'Brent Bravo' oil production platform in the Brent oil field. [*September 1976*]

139

139 *Iron Lady goes heavy metal*

Three years before she started her three terms as Prime Minister, Conservative Party leader Margaret Thatcher was already known as the "Iron Maiden" by the Russians after her warning on the buildup of Soviet naval power. Here she becomes acquainted with another heavy metal proponent of the Cold War arms struggle – the Polaris submarine HMS Revenge – under the tutelage of CPO Coxn Southward. [*November 1976*]

140 *Poles fail to repel boarders*

Twelve foreign trawlers – including four Soviet vessels pictured here – were boarded by the minesweeper HMS Cuxton during a three-day patrol in and around the Bristol Channel.

Three Polish trawlers, two each from Belgium and Spain, and one from France were among the remainder visited. Though ever vigilant for infringements of fishery regulations, Navy men were often able to maintain cordial relations during these inspections – as when a Cuxton party looked over the Polish fishery training ship Rybak Moreski and was entertained to lunch on board. [*January 1977*]

140

141

142

141 *Trompe-l'oeil after Wild Thyme*

HMS Fearless seems to be carrying out an awkward manoeuvre during her visit to Venice – but there was more distance between her bridge and the elegant span in the foreground than appears in this photograph...

Earlier in her Mediterranean deployment 846 Naval Air Squadron took part in Exercise Wild Thyme off Malta – and B Flight celebrated their 1,000th deck landing. [*January 1977*]

142 *Craggy Churchill*

The Rock sets off the lines of the nuclear Fleet submarine HMS Churchill as she prepares to enter Gibraltar in this photograph taken by LA(Phot) R Dobson of HMS Tiger. [*March 1977*]

143 **Maid of all work**

A grand old lady bows out – HMS Maidstone, an accommodation ship for 2,000 troops in Northern Ireland since November 1969, leaves Belfast Docks on her final journey to Rosyth to be scrapped.

Launched in 1938, she had started life as a submarine depot ship. Between 1958 and 1962 she was extensively reconstructed as a support ship for nuclear powered submarines. During her Northern Ireland years, she dropped the HMS prefix and came under Army direction. A naval party maintained the ship's services. [*April 1977*]

144 **Sabre dance**

HMS Sabre cuts a dash at an international gathering at Portland. The fast training boat is pictured sweeping past HMS Juno (left) and her Wasp helicopter; HNLMS Friesland (centre) of the Royal Netherlands Navy; and (right) the Nigerian Navy's corvette Otobo. [*May 1977*]

143

144

145

145 Relics returned to Rodney

Sea King helicopters of 826 Squadron embarked in HMS Tiger were employed to lift a 200-year-old 32 pounder cannon to Fort Rodney, 350ft above sea level on Pigeon Island in the Caribbean.

The fort, under restoration by the St Lucia Historical and Archaeological Society, was named after Admiral Lord Rodney, whose fleet defeated the French at the Battle of the Saintes in 1782. The cannon had been removed from the island in the 19th century and the Defence Adviser Nassau – in charge of naval operations in the Caribbean – was asked if the Royal Navy could help replace them. The Tiger was leading a task group that included the nuclear Fleet submarine HMS Churchill and the frigates Jupiter, Aurora, Euryalus, Ariadne, Danae and Antelope, on their way home from a transatlantic deployment via West African ports after visits to Brazil, Venezuala and Argentina. [*May 1977*]

146

146 Old Battle signs off with Old Glory

The 3,835 ton sonar trials ship HMS Matapan enters Portsmouth Harbour for the last time, her paying off pennant suspended from a large balloon, together with the Stars and Stripes, representing the American involvement in her final programme. A former Battle class destroyer, she was completed in 1947 and then spent 20 years in Reserve before a two-year conversion to her new role, which began in 1973. [*August 1977*]

147 **Taylor-made ski-jump**

Trials on the ski-jump – a Harrier leaves the test ramp, set at six degrees, on the runway at RAE Bedford. Lieut.-Cdr Doug Taylor had the idea of curving up the front of a flight deck runway so that the aircraft could be launched on an upward trajectory. When raised to 20 degrees, this facility would allow a Harrier to carry more than 2,000 lb of extra fuel and weapons – and afford increased safety margins for a pilot forced to make a snap decision to eject in the event of a malfunction on take-off.

Ramps were already being planned for HMS Invincible, first of the Royal Navy's new "through-deck cruisers" and HMS Illustrious, currently in build on the Tyne. [*November 1977*]

147

148 **Jenny bridges the generations**

Jenny and her side party, after completing their usual excellent paint job on HMS Amazon, were joined on her sampan by the Type 21 frigate's commanding officer Cdr Bruce Richardson, First Lieutenant Lieut.-Cdr Bill Hutchison, and the buffer, PO Monty Stockham. Jenny had painted ships for Stockham's father – but was not sure if his HMS Kent was the one with three funnels or four... [*February 1978*]

148

149 **Rover's Return visit**

HMS Hardy, last of the Type 14 frigates, moors at Runcorn to allow a small freighter to pass her on the Manchester Ship Canal. The ship, which had just paid off to the Reserve Squadron, was flagship to the Flag Officer Plymouth (Vice Admiral John Forbes) when he made a six day visit to the city. Highlight of the stay was a by now traditional call to Granada TV studios, where a party of sailors met the stars of "Coronation Street" in the Rover's Return. [*May 1978*]

149

150

151

150 Robust answer to a big problem

The RMAS tug Robust lends a hand to HMS Ark Royal as she leaves Devonport at the start of her final deployment. When the supertanker Amoco Cadiz spewed thousands of tons of oil into the Channel and onto the Britanny coast, Robust helped carry out a dispersal blitz on the northern edge of the slick, saving beaches in the south of England from the threat of massive pollution. [*June 1978*]

151 Gannets gather over Morayshire

By pooling their resources, 849 Squadron and B Flight managed to produce nine Gannets to fly in formation over the major towns in Morayshire as a farewell salute before B Flight's final embarkation in HMS Ark Royal. [*June 1978*]

152 No chimes at midnight

There were no cheering crowds for HMS Southampton when the Royal Navy's latest guided missile destroyer glided down her covered slipway in Vosper Thornycroft's Woolston shipyard at Southampton.

Following industrial action by the yard's Boilermakers Union members the ship was launched in secret just before midnight on January 29 – if the tide had been missed it might have been months before the already postponed launching could have taken place.

Earlier that day the Type 42 was named at a VIP ceremony in the shipyard's giant covered building complex. But because of industrial action, the Southampton remained firmly on her slipway after Lady Cameron, wife of Marshal of the Royal Air Force Sir Neil Cameron, Chief of the Defence Staff, had christened her with champagne. [*March 1979*]

153 Jetstream observer

First Sea Lord Admiral Sir Terry Lewin was one of the first passengers in the Navy's newest aircraft, the turboprop Jetstream T2, when he flew on a visit to the RN air station Culdrose.

The Jetstream had taken over the observer training role from the piston engined Sea Prince, which had served for 25 years. [*May 1979*]

152

153

154 Deep sea space shuttle

The Royal Navy and the United States Navy achieved the first underwater "space shuttle" type link-up between two dived submarines when men from HMS Odin were ferried to HMS Repulse using the American deep submergence rescue vehicle (DSRV) Avalon.

During the exercise the Odin, a diesel/electric conventional submarine, acted as an accident victim, lying 400 ft down off the Isle of Arran, Western Scotland. The Polaris submarine Repulse was the mother vessel for Avalon. Acting on a simulated "subsunk" distress call, the 50ft long 37 ton Avalon was flown to Glasgow from her base at San Diego in a giant Lockheed Galaxy and transported by road to the Clyde Submarine Base where she was loaded pick-a-back fashion onto the after casing of the Repulse.

The "nuke" duly sailed and released Avalon to search for the Odin. Visibility was down to a few feet – but contact was made using sonar and Avalon attached herself exactly over the escape hatch – and thus men from the Odin were able to climb into the Avalon to be transferred to the Repulse without getting their feet wet. [*June 1979*]

155

154

155 **Numb chums**

Bang, you're wet! Informal farewells were a feature of life in Standing Naval Force Atlantic patrols, ranging from slogans trailed from helicopters to the release of multitudes of coloured balloons. On this occasion HMS Ariadne trained her 4.5 inch gun turret and let go with jets of water as she steamed past Canadian Commodore G L Edwart Edwards in HMCS Iroquois before he handed over the squadron to Captain Gerald Carter, USN.

Ariadne's time within the Arctic Circle had entitled her to temporarily acquire a painted blue nose and her officers and men to be awarded certificates of membership of the Society of Numb Friends as she spent five weeks in Norwegian waters, taking part in multi-national exercises and visiting the ports of Tromso, Haakonsvern, Stavanger and Kristiansand before returning to the North Sea. [*July 1979*]

156

156 **Guardship in Gay Paree**

HMS Thornham, the inshore minesweeper attached to Aberdeen University RN unit, was paying a three-day visit to Paris with midshipman students embarked – after acting as guardship at the scene of salvage work on the German tanker Tarpenbek, which sank off the Isle of Wight after a collision. [*September 1979*]

157 **On top of old Snakey**

A Babary ape gets a rock-top view of HMS Blake alongside in Gibraltar. 'Old Snakey' was having a final fling in the Mediterranean before returning to port for the last time. The old lady proved she was still full of life by maintaining 30 knots during full power trials west of Corsica. [*December 1979*]

157

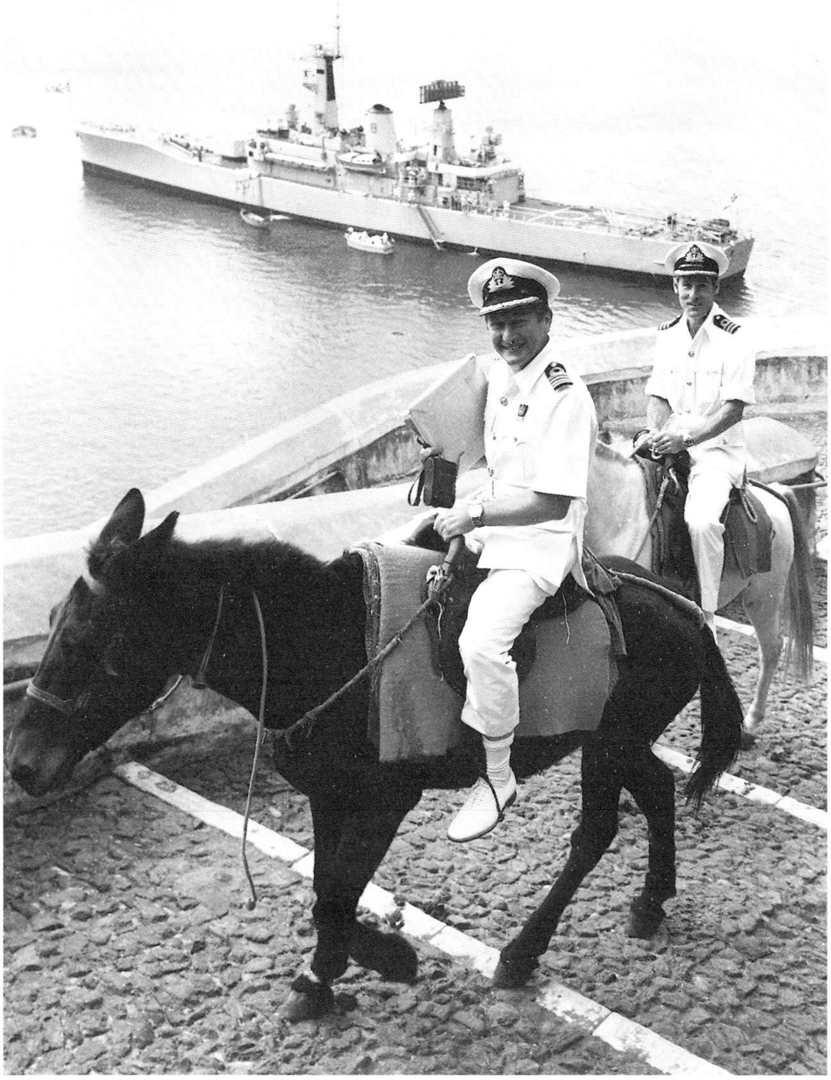

158

159

158 *Sure-footed friends*

Heehaw, me hearties... Not very dignified, perhaps, but when HM ships Ajax and Scylla arrived at the island of Thira (Santorini) north of Crete, everybody wanted a donkey ride once they discovered it was the only easy way to climb the 700 ft volcanic cliff to the village. Here the ships' commanding officers, Capt. Mike Rawlinson (Ajax) and Cdr Jake Backus (Scylla) make the ascent to deliver presents to the island's mayor.

159 *Wild and woolly Jersey*

The Island class offshore patrol vessels had earned a reputation for moving about a bit in heavy seas – but HMS Jersey was built to Merchant Navy standards and boasted a comfort and spaciousness of living accommodation that invited comparison with a floating hotel...

Jersey and her sister ship Alderney had been taken to the hearts of the Channel Islands that gave them their names – lifting morale and leaving a fund of goodwill to sustain them in their tough fishery protection tasks.

Just before a visit to St Helier, the Jersey was involved in a North Sea chase when a Danish trawler refused to stop. The Jersey had put a three-man boarding party on the vessel for a routine inspection, but the skipper set out for his home port, defying an order to put into Grimsby. HMS Jersey fired two warning shots and eventually the trawler turned for the UK – after the Jersey called up a frigate to assist. [*January 1980*]

160 *Shadowlands*

Shadowing the Russians could be a chilly business – as HMS Leander found in the Soviet Arctic exercise areas. As the Russian carrier Kiev led her task force home, the Leander was waiting for her amid the ice pack of the Kola inlet, isolated from the NATO forces following the group. [*July 1980*]

F109

161

161 Liverpool's Dee lords it at Liege

HMS Dee experienced one of her proudest moments when the 142-ton tender of the Royal Naval Unit at Liverpool University was chosen to lead a three-nation flotilla through Liege to celebrate the Belgian city's millenium.

The Dee, which this year celebrated her own 25th birthday, was chosen because her size made it possible for her to negotiate the Albert Canal from Antwerp without difficulty.

Highlight of the visit was when more than 200 craft – barges, tugs and larger vessels – steamed along the River Meuse past the Prince of Liege who took the salute. Before the celebration the Royal Navy contingent joined with the ships companies of the Belgian Navy patrol craft Schelde and Semois and the French ship Dahlia in a wreath-laying service at the grave of one of the founder members of the Belgian Force Navale – formed during the Second World War under RN tutelage.

163

162 Nothing serious

VT2 P234, the Royal Navy's largest hovercraft, operates close to an underwater explosion in a trial that would have seriously damaged a conventional displacement vessel of comparable size.

Normally, only unmanned craft destined for scrap would have been exposed to a detonation of such intensity – but here the crew reported only a slight bump under their feet and the craft returned to her base at the RN Hovercraft Trials Unit at Lee-on-Solent with all systems working. Designed and built by Vosper Thornycroft, she was being evaluated for mine countermeasures work.

162

163 Invincible gets watered down

HMS Invincible, first of the Royal Navy's new class carriers, during pre-wetting trials in the North Sea. She was soon off to Gibraltar for a self-maintenance period and then carried out the first engine change for an embarked Sea Harrier before more trials in the Western Approaches. [*November 1980*]

164 Cradled in the creek

Another submarine survivor that would form the basis of the new Submarine Museum complex at Gosport was HMS Alliance, last of the World War II type submarines to serve in the Royal Navy.

Raised nestling in concrete cradles on massive piles buried deep in Haslar Creek at Gosport – home of the Submarine Service's Alma Mater, HMS Dolphin – at the end of a unique and complex civil engineering operation, the 36-year-old boat would have two aircraft-type doors cut in her sides to allow easy on-off access by the visiting public. [*July 1981*]

164

165

165 *Southern star*

HMS Leeds Castle, first of the new class of offshore patrol vessels designed for the protection of national assets of fish, gas and oil within the 200-mile limit, was due for acceptance.

Fitted with a 40/60 Bofors gun and able to operate a Sea King helicopter, she and her sister HMS Dunbarton Castle would give sterling service for long periods much further afield – in the South Atlantic. [*August 1981*]

166 *Poole's Black Pig*

The "Black Pig", with its distinctive camouflage and heated glass fibre "igloo" – this "arcticised" landing craft had been sailed from Scotland to Norway for Exercise Cold Soak, to test the ability of an LCU (Landing Craft Utility) to operate unprotected during harsh northern winter conditions.

It was the first time one had crossed the North Sea under its own power. LCUs operating in Norway had hitherto done so from heated facilities on board amphibious ships or at the dockside. The Black Pig – so called because of its unusual dark brown and black livery – was largely independent.

Based at Poole, it was due to return to the UK at the end of the annual Royal Marines Arctic deployment. [*November 1981*]

166

167

167 Recorders at record strength

For 75 years one of the smallest sub-specialist branches of the Royal Navy had been getting the measure of the world – with 140 ratings, the Survey Recorders Branch was at record strength, having increased its complement six-fold since formation in January, 1907.

In an anniversary feature Navy News noted that, for its size, it was one of the most widely-spread branches in the Fleet, working continually in such far-flung places as the Middle East, Antartica and the West Indies.

The role of the survey recorder embraced both hydrographic and oceanographic work – the latter undertaken by the Royal Navy's larger survey ships – such as HMS Hecla, seen here. [*May 1982*]

168

169

168 Hermes heads the Task Force

Pictured here, her deck packed with Sea Harriers and Sea Kings ready for action – HMS Hermes leaves for the South Atlantic, heading the Falklands Task Force. An emotional wave of tears and pride – not to mention the strains of the carrier anthem, Rod Stewart's "Sailing" – attended the venerable Hermes' departure after a week-end of feverish preparation that followed the news of Argentina's invasion of the Falkland Islands. The huge effort to bring together men, stores, provisions and ammunition was quickly appreciated in Captain Linley Middleton's signal: "The commanding officer, officers and ship's company of HMS Hermes would like to pass to the City of Portsmouth, the Naval Base and Royal Dockyard, their heartfelt thanks for the magnificent co-operation and goodwill that sped them on their way so expeditiously..." [*May 1982*]

169 Tribals out of the reservation

Three Tribal Class frigates were brought out of the Standby Squadron to enjoy a new lease of life, plugging the gaps left in escort forces as a result of the Falklands conflict.

HMS Gurkha – seen here sailing from Rosyth for sea trials – was joined by HM ships Tartar and Zulu, all first commissioned in 1962-64, working up to once more become operational members of the Fleet.

Among the guests at the Gurkha's commissioning was the Army's only serving VC, Capt. Rambahadur Limbu of the Gurkhas who won the highest award for valour in action as a sergeant during the Borneo campaign in 1965. [*September 1982*]

170 Peace mission

"Sea Power for Peace" was the farewell message from Polaris submarine HMS Resolution to well-wishers on the jetty at the Clyde Submarine Base as she paid off to go into a two-year refit at Rosyth. Resolution flipped open her missile hatches to reveal the words as she sailed down the Gareloch with 39 operational patrols behind her. [*October 1982*]

170

171 Hats on in Hermes

HMS Hermes helped launch TV-am's breakfast show "Good Morning Britain" when 500 members of the ship's company formed the word 'Britain' on the flight deck.

The TV-am camera crew were in a Wessex helicopter filming the "off caps" drill for the opening titles of the new programme. In a painstaking two-day operation, the title was completed by 5,000 West Country villagers forming "Good" and pigeons in Trafalgar Square, bribed with birdseed to spell out "Morning". [*February 1983*]

172 Freedom of entry for Exeter

Forty-three years after the founding of the Fifth Destroyer Flotilla of K-Class ships under Lord Mountbatten in HMS Kelly, the "Fighting Fifth" was reborn with the Fifth Destroyer Squadron – the five Type 42 destroyers HMS Southampton, Nottingham, Liverpool, Manchester and Exeter. The Exeter seen here had already earned the "fighting" tag, having acquitted herself with distinction in the Falklands war when she was largely responsible for repelling an Exocet attack on May 30, 1982. She had just been accorded the highest honour of the city whose name she bore – the Freedom of Entry to Exeter. [*February 1983*]

172

171

173

173 **Hecate's grey days**

HMS Hecate returned to Devonport at the end of a deployment to the South Atlantic during which she spent 174 days continuously at sea or in exposed anchorages – a record for an ocean survey ship – and was the first such vessel to circumnavigate the South American continent.

Sent south the previous July to relieve the ice patrol ship HMS Endurance, she had been fitted with armaments to equip her for her new role and her smart white livery was painted over grey.

After briefings at Port Stanley she had sailed through heavy seas to South Georgia to take up her ice patrol duties and to survey virgin seabed exposed by receding glaciers. Embarked were Army and British Antarctic Survey personnel who were to inspect damage caused by the Argentines to the scientific station at Grytviken and the derelict whaling station.

Between regular troop transport and support passages from South Georgia to the Falklands, the Hecate made major surveys of uncharted areas, often in atrocious conditions. But the seas were flat calm when she was pictured here surveying Mare Harbour. [*March 1983*]

174

174 Learning the three 'Ms'

Ambling along at a few knots, three of the smallest ships in the Royal Navy had become familiar sights in the waters off Plymouth. HMS Manly, Mentor and Milbrook started work the previous year as seagoing classrooms for new entry trainees at HMS Raleigh. They had replaced the inshore MCM craft previously employed by Raleigh – HM ships Dittisham, Flintham and Aveley. [*May 1983*]

176 Orkney loses Linda Louise

HMS Orkney succeeded in extinguishing a fire on board an abandoned fishing boat off the Yorkshire coast, only for the vessel to founder as she prepared to take her in tow.

Humber Coastguard asked the Orkney to assist the blazing Linda Louise 45 miles east of Bridlington. Her crew had been winched to safety the previous day by an RAF helicopter, and a rig support vessel, the Saint Kitts, had abandoned a tow when the fire reignited.

The Orkney found the Linda Louise ablaze from deck house to stern; with sea conditions so bad it was impossible to get firefighters onto her. To reach the flames she had to lay herself alongside, bow to stern, and fight the fire from the fo'c'sle.

This meant the firefighters were sometimes engulfed in acrid smoke and were in some danger from the fishing boat's derricks. Having put the fire out, the Orkney prepared to take up the tow. But the Linda Louise had been taking a lot of water over her stern ramp into her exposed engine room, and she foundered and plunged to the bottom. [*August 1983*]

176

175 **Schooled for War**

Gun-line exercises reminiscent of the Falklands War were enacted by Royal Navy frigates – including HMS Ariadne here leading a line with HM ships Torquay, Apollo, Liverpool and Alacrity – for the first Staff College Sea Days held off Portsmouth for four years.

A special audience of 800 drawn from military staff colleges, schools and foreign navies watched the action. [*July 1983*]

175

177

177 *Illustrious takes to Manhattan*

A Sea King helicopter of 814 Naval Air Squadron hovers over the Statue of Liberty during HMS Illustrious's visit to New York. While her sister ship Invincible was basking in the Australian summer sunshine, the Illustrious was heading for sub-zero temperatures – which did little to chill their reception in the "Big-Apple". During her six-day stay the Stateside welcome was almost overwhelming as she was deluged with personal offers of hospitality from New Yorkers, sightseeing tours, skiing, skating, sports fixtures and excursions into Manhattan's vibrant night life.

Among those who visited the ship was the famous New York Jets football team, who took on an Illustrious team at basketball – the professional sportsmen winning by a narrow margin of 62–54. [*March 1984*]

178 *Early birds give warning*

Spanning a generation of airborne early warning aircraft in the Royal Navy, this pair highlighted the resurgence of AEW in the Fleet Air Arm.

The veteran Fairey Gannet was the last example of its kind flying with the FAA and represented a type which entered service 23 years before. It was flown here by Lieut.-Cdr Ken Lamprey, former senior pilot of the last operational Gannet flight. Its AEW role with 849 Squadron ended with the paying off of HMS Ark Royal in 1978 – now it was used in noise trials from RN air station Culdrose.

The Sea King was of an AEW type hastily developed during the Falklands war and formed part of the new 849 Squadron due to be recomissioned once up to strength with its crews fully trained. [*December 1983*]

178

179 **Achilles sees red**

The Leander frigate HMS Achilles had been seeing a lot of the Soviet Navy in recent weeks, prompted at very short notice by one of the biggest Russian naval exercises for years. She was operating under the control of Commodore Clyde when she was ordered to rendezvous with RFA Grey Rover in Moray Firth before setting out to shadow the Russian fleet.

She first spent 48 hours on the tail of a Juliet class cruise missile submarine leaving the Skagerrak. There were more than 50 major Soviet units at sea, including a high proportion of ballistic missile submarines, and the Achilles soon found herself on the trail of other warships well inside the Arctic Circle. In a series of high-speed dashes, both frigate and RFA kept close watch on three Krivak frigates and a Kydna cruiser all the way to North Cape.

The Achilles had earlier been involved in surveillance duties while on passage to take up her Gibraltar guardship role. Here she takes a close look at a Soviet Udaloy class vessel as it heads for the Gibraltar Straits while escorting the helicopter cruiser Leningrad. [*May 1984*]

179

180

182

180 Brief respite for Warspite

Although HMS Warspite had completed three Falkland patrols, it was only during her most recent spell in the South Atlantic that many of her crew were able to step onto the territory they had spent so long defending.

The 90 day deployment finally included a run ashore when the nuclear powered Fleet submarine visited the forward repair ship Bar Protector, a vessel taken up from trade, in San Carlos Water to collect mail and stores. [*May 1984*]

181

181 Beach crowds get a blast out of Sandpiper

HMS Sandpiper was often visiting South Coast ports in her training role for Britannia Royal Naval College, Dartmouth – but she seldom got the chance to open fire on them ... Here she "bombards" Weymouth beach during a 40th anniversary D-Day re-enactment – in company with HMS Stubbington and warships from several other nations.

With battle ensigns flying and flares and rockets going off in salvoes, the ships put on a fine show for the large crowd watching from the beach. After the defences had been suitably softened up, an amphibious assault was carried out by Royal Marines and Royal Engineers. [*July 1984*]

183 Uncommonly cold – even in the Baltic

HMS Arethusa and her Standing Naval Force Atlantic colleagues could have been forgiven a sniffle or two when they ran into some of the coldest Baltic temperatures on record.

Arctic weather during her last few weeks with the NATO squadron – nicknamed "Sniffle" because of its initials – ensured the British frigate a freezing farewell and caused a sneeze in the Force's programme.

A planned visit to Copenhagen had to be cancelled because of thick pack ice in the area, while ship's divers had to skate over plans to exercise in Den Helder when the harbour froze solid overnight. [*April 1985*]

183

182 A brace of birds for Hong Kong

Offshore patrol vessels HMS Peacock (leading) and HMS Plover leave Portsmouth on the first leg of their long voyage to Hong Kong.

The first two replacement vessels for the elderly ships of the Hong Kong Squadron were due to reach the Crown Colony in late November. Later they would be joined by the other ships of the class, Swallow, Swift and Starling.

The 700-tonne vessels built by Hall Russell of Aberdeen would carry out patrol duties against smugglers and illegal immigrants as well as search and rescue and other operations. [*October 1984*]

184 Stepping out

"On the step" during the Westlant deployment is the nuclear-powered Fleet submarine HMS Warspite. This involved riding on her own bow wave, providing maximum speed on the surface when fast transit passage was required – operationally, of course, nuclear submarines are seldom required to break surface.

The Warspite had just completed a 79-day Stateside cruise, during which she carried out a series of trials at the American Underwater Undersea Test and Evaluation Centre (AUTEC) range by Andros Island in the Bahamas.

Other units involved were Nimrod aircraft of 42 and 120 Squadrons, Sea King helicopters of 824 Squadron, HM submarine Spartan – and HMS Plymouth, from which this picture was taken. [*July 1985*]

184

185 Links with Arks of old

HMS Ark Royal approaches Semaphore Tower and HMS Cardiff on her first entry to Portsmouth Naval Base. Vantage points in HMS Dolphin, the submarine base on the east side of the harbour entrance, and HMS Vernon were lined with Service personnel waiting to greet the new carrier that had inherited the Royal Navy's most glamorous warship name – while thousands of spectators gathered on the beaches of Southsea and the walls of Old Portsmouth to cheer her in.

Drawn up on her flight deck were a Swordfish and a Sea Harrier, both of them links with Arks of old – the 'Stringbag' for its connections with the Second World War carrier, the Sea Harrier (the first fixed wing aircraft to land on the new Ark) because it was piloted by Lieut-.-Cdr Hugh Slade, last man to land a fixed wing aircraft on the present ship's immediate predecessor. Slade, commanding officer of 899 Naval Air Squadron, flew from Yeovilton to join the ship off the Nab Tower.

Although completed months ahead of schedule at a cost of £320m, the Fleet's biggest, newest and costliest acquisition carried 250 Tyneside shipbuilders on her acceptance voyage – some of them staying on board to complete unfinished painting and other minor jobs. As she went through powered roll manouvres on the way down through the North Sea, a lone "Mrs Mop" was still doggedly swabbing the uppermost decks after 211 personnel had been ordered below. [*August 1985*]

185

186

187

186 **River passage to Canada**
HMS Dovey leads HMS Waveney and HMS Carron through Camso locks on their passage across Nova Scotia. The three new River class vessels manned entirely by RNR crews were on a six week deployment to Canada arranged to coincide with the 75th anniversary celebrations of the Royal Canadian Navy. Each took three different crews, with changeovers taking place at the end of the passage to Canada and again before the return.

More than 30 warships from a dozen different countries had converged on Bedford Basin, Halifax – including HMS Brilliant in company with her Standing Naval Force Atlantic partners, HMS Alacrity, HM submarine Sealion and RFA Gold Rover. Lieut The Prince Andrew reviewed the Fleet. [*August 1985*]

187 **The daring Duchess**
During an afternoon spent dived off Plymouth The Duchess of Kent watched emergency surface drills and travelled back to Devonport perched high on the fin of HMS Turbulent with the nuclear submarine's commanding officer, Cdr Tim Lightoller.

The Duchess, who had lunch on board, took a particular interest in the welfare of the crew during her tour of the new boat. [*November 1985*]

188 **No baby boomer**

Fine shot of a big shot – and one to stir memories for generations of matelots. The mighty United States battleship USS Iowa fired a broadside in the South West Approaches as a finale to the NATO exercise Ocean Safari. Witnesses on board the Type 22 frigate HMS Brilliant (foreground) reported a blinding orange flash, a searing blast of heat and a shock wave to stun the senses as the 16 inch guns roared out. The whine of the one ton practice shells could be heard for several seconds before. With a series of dull underwater booms, they broke up on hitting the water, sending up huge plumes of spray.

The Iowa, laid down in 1940, had been reactivated and extensively modernised to carry a mighty armoury of other weapons, including up-to-date missiles. With her sisters New Jersey, Missouri and Wisconsin, she was among the largest battleships ever built – only the Japanese Yamato and Musashi were bigger. [*November 1985*]

189

189 **A deliberate shock to the system**

HMS Invincible appeared to have suffered a terrible fate. Actually the cloud of smoke and spray came from a carefully controlled explosion in the Solent mining ground where the carrier was exposed to a series of first-of-class shock trials to test the effectiveness of her equipment and machinery in a wartime environment. Since she commissioned in 1980 the Invincible had sailed over 260,000 miles and was now entering a long refit at Devonport. [*May 1986*]

190 **Malta besieges Brazen**

An armada of tiny vessels accompanies HMS Brazen as she arrives in Grand Harbour, Valletta at the start of the first visit by a Royal Navy warship to Malta for seven years. During her five day call a tenth of the island's population – 30,000 people – visited her. When she sailed she took with her for scattering at sea the ashes of Ernle Bradford, the eminent naval historian who had written of the island's two great sieges – by the Turks in the days of the Knights of St John and by the Axis powers in World War II that had earned Malta the award of the George Cross. [*October 1986*]

190

191

191 Fast recovery

When the 2,000 tonne Taiwanese freighter Kwang Ta developed a heavy list 200 miles off Hong Kong HMS Swift came to the rescue. The freighter's cargo of scrap metal and engine parts had shifted in rough weather, causing a 60 degree cant to starboard and forcing her to shut down her main engines. Unable to lower life rafts or boats, the ship's master put out a distress call which was answered by the Swift and a Titan aircraft of the Royal Hong Kong Auxiliary Air Force.

By the time the patrol craft arrived, 25 members of the Kwang Ta's crew had been rescued by an oil rig support vessel, but eight remained on board. A Sea Rider was detached to pick them up – but as it stood off between the Swift and the Kwang Ta, it was hit by a hugh wave and capsized, throwing ABs Gillgrass and Kiu-sang into the sea. The men crawled back onto the upturned Sea Rider and, because the Swift was rolling so heavily, were able to step from the boat onto the patrol craft's deck.

The severity of the Kwang's Ta's list is graphically illustrated by this photograph, taken after the freighter had entered the safe waters of Junk Bay, with HMS Swift on the left. [*February 1987*]

192 Superb feat at the Pole

Standing like dark sentinels in the white wastes of the Arctic ice-cap, these three nuclear-powered submarines were logging one more entry in the record books of the North Pole.

It was the first time that British and American submarines had surfaced together at the top of the world – and honours were shared by the Fleet hunter-killer boat HMS Superb (furthest from the camera) USS Billfish and USS Sea Devil.

The unique event gave both navies the opportunity to work closely together in refining submarine tactics in the world's harshest and most exacting maritime environment.

HMS Superb was commanded by Cdr Jeff Collins – the first former rating to be given command of a 'nuke'. [*July 1987*]

192

193 **Orwell off Catalonia**

Looking neatly aggressive, HMS Orwell leads the rest of the Tenth Mine countermeasures Squadron towards Gibraltar – HMS Spey, Arun, Itchen, Ribbie, Humber and Helford following behind.

Over 500 officers and men of the Royal Naval Reserve were taking part in exercises in the Mediterranean, embarked in the seven River Class minesweepers. [*August 1987*]

194 **In the heat of the day – and night**

HMS Active passes the tanker Lanistes in the scorching heat of the Gulf. The Royal Navy's long-standing Armilla Patrols here covered the height of the Gulf's searing summer temperatures – soaring to more than 45 degrees C (113 F) and often above 35 degrees at midnight. While on station in the Gulf of Oman and the Arabian Gulf, scores of transits were made in the Strait of Hormuz – Active alone made 38, accompanying nearly 3.6 million tons of shipping. [*September 1987*]

193

194

195

195 Yellow peril

A "yellow submarine" was going to work with the Gulf Group, using a TV eye. After several weeks of finding a huge range of objects – including oil drums, rusting bicycles and dead sheep – the RN minehunters operating in the Gulf area disposed of a number of mines. HMS Brecon discovered one 300 feet down on the sea bed and sent her miniature submersible to investigate. Back to the ship came the picture outline of a horned mine – and later four more were located and destroyed.

Here, rafted up alongside the support ship Abdiel are the minehunters Brecon, Brocklesby and Bicester, with the frigate HMS Andromeda keeping a watchful eye. [*November 1987*]

196

196 Watching each other

For the first time since the Falklands War, the Royal Navy was weighing up the lesson to be learned from a large-scale, non-NATO exercise by combined forces. With many of the problems of the South Atlantic conflict built into its scenario, Exercise Purple Warrior tested the capability of carrier-borne aircraft, warships and seaborne troops to rescue British nationals from islands under foreign invasion.

The fictitious 'Kaig' group of islands were, in reality, the Mulls of Kintyre and Galloway and the Isle of Arran; the evacuees were played by volunteers from among the local people. Command ship for the task group within the amphibious operations area was the assault ship HMS Intrepid – with a Warsaw Pact observer taking a turn on the wheel of one of her landing craft. He was there by invitation as part of an agreement signed in Stockholm in 1986.

Meanwhile the destroyer HMS Liverpool was in the Barents Sea watching – without invitation – Russian vessels such as this Alfa Class nuclear-powered attack submarine emerging from a smoke screen laid by a Soviet surface warship.

The picture was taken from the Liverpool's helicopter during joint gunnery and missile firings by Russia's Northern Fleet and air units. [*January 1988*]

197 Colour co-ordinates

The new colour scheme of the Lynx helicopter motivated this picture of HMS York's flight taken by LA(Phot) Michael 'Dutchy' Mulholland. HMS Ark Royal is seen below entering Portland Harbour. [*February 1988*]

198 Minelayer with a mind of her own

HMS Abdiel, the Navy's only surface minelayer, paid off after 21 years' service. A ship with the reputation of having a mind of her own, her wilful ways were recalled by one of her former commanding officers, the Queen's Harbourmaster at Portsmouth Captain Dick Smith: "Once I was trying to turn her stern into the wind and she wouldn't have it – and my navigating officer whispered in my ear. 'Look, sir, she wants to go the other way – why not let her get on with it?"

The Abdiel's last role was in support of minehunters in the Gulf. [*June 1988*]

197

198

199 **Helping hand for HMY**

For the first time in her 34-year career, HMY Britannia had taken on fuel from a foreign fleet oiler while under way.

Two replenishments at sea were performed with the American ship Andrew J Higgins as the yacht headed for Australia to take part in the bicentennial celebrations. The first RAS – the Americans call them underway replenishments or "unreps" – took place between Southern California and Hawaii, the second as the Britannia left Hawaii for Australia. [*August 1988*]

199

200

201

200 **Ambuscade in the aftermath of Gilbert**

West Indies guardship HMS Ambuscade, serenely Med-moored in Gran Cayman. The stern-to-jetty positioning was and is a practice more common to liners in the Mediterranean, where tidal considerations are not so important.

In stark contrast, her successor in the guardship role, HMS Active, had been lately living up to her name in disaster relief work – speeding to assist in the wake one of the deceptively tranquil Caribbean's worst hurricanes of the century.

She was at Maracaibo, Venezuela when warnings of Hurricane Gilbert were flashed out in the previous month. In the Cayman Islands the Type 21 frigate found huge seas crashing on shore and working parties were flown in to help clear debris and disentangle power lines.

But when it became clear that damage in Jamaica was on a much greater scale, the Active and RFA Orangeleaf made best speed to Kingston – to find much of the island devastated, with thousands homeless and shocked, power and water supplies cut, and crops wiped out.

Soon the ship's company were busy re-roofing and cleaning up hospitals and rehabilitation centres – while the cooks were providing the hungry populace with their first hot meal – stew and rice for 6,000 was the order.

While medical teams became expert at administering anti-tetanus injections and dealing with cuts and abrasions, the ship's helicopter flew out supplies to outlying clinics and the navigation officer carried out a survey of Kingston Harbour, checking on beacons and buoys which had been dragged out of position by the force of the winds. [*October 1988*]

201 **Campbeltown has her bell back**

On contractor's sea trials off the Scottish coast, the new Type 22 Batch 3 frigate HMS Campbeltown would soon commission, carrying the bell of her famous predecessor of St Nazaire fame.

Residents of Campbeltown, Pennsylvania, where the 50lb brass bell had been cared for by the local fire company since 1950, had voted for its return to the new holder of a distinguished name. (*December 1988*)

202 **On gossamer wings**

Was this the first time that a microlight aircraft had been flown from an aircraft carrier at sea? Six flights were conducted from HMS Illustrious by 42-year old David Garrison from Cambridgeshire as the ship headed home from its western Atlantic deployment.

On two of them the intrepid visitor offered to take passengers in the two-seater Pegaus Q aircraft, which has a cruising speed of 70 mph and a 250 mile range. So far the Ministry of Defence has failed to take advantage of the microlight's low radar signature potentialities as a spotter – though towed hang gliders once had their uses, deployed by submarines. It was not a popular duty – the observer always had the uncomfortable impression that, once he had made a sighting, the tow line might be released to give the submarine its best chance of making a covert approach to its target. [*February 1989*]

203

205 **Broader in the beam**

Showing off her new-look, hull-strengthening beams is the "stretched" Type 42 Batch 3 destroyer HMS Gloucester, operating on trials off the Isle of Wight.

The beams – at deck edge level and extending from the gun to the flight deck – were installed as part of a five-month DED at Portsmouth Naval Base.

The whole package of work had increased the ship's displacement by about 150 tonnes – while the beams made her about two feet wider overall. [*March 1989*]

206 **Stretched dock**

The Type 22 frigate HMS Boxer enters the newly extended No 6 Dock in the Frigate Refitting Complex at Devonport. She was the first ship to move into the central dock, which had been lengthened by 12 metres to accommodate the "stretched" Type 22s and the Type 23 Duke Class frigates for refits under cover. A new sonar pit funded by NATO had also been built into the dock. [*December 1989*]

203 **Sandown sails**

HMS Sandown, first of the new class of single-role minehunters, on her contractor's sea trials in the Solent – out for the first time from her builders, Vosper Thornycroft.

204 **Three of the Third**

Eagle-eyed enthusiasts at the Clyde Submarine Base, Faslane were treated to a rare sight when representatives of all three classes of submarine in the Third Submarine Squadron took to the water.

Churchill Class HMS Courageous (in foreground), Oberon Class HMS Odin (middle) and Swiftsure Class HMS Sceptre were heading out on manoeuvres. [*March 1989*]

204

205

206

207 Trophy winner
A striking aerial view of the new Type 22 frigate HMS Cumberland operating off Portland won the Maritime Trophy for PO(Phot) Mike Mitchell. [*January 1990*]

208 Nosey Ocelot
Meanwhile a winning shot in the black and white section of the annual Peregrine Trophy photographic competition was LA(Phot) Jon Garthwaite's unusual bows-on view of the conventional diesel electric submarine HMS Ocelot, showing off her new streamlined sonar dome. [*January 1990*]

209 Tracking down the Triads
Smuggling in one form or another – drugs, illegal immigrants, electronic equipment – was proving to be a lucrative proposition on the other side of the globe. HMS Plover's fast pursuit craft shows the form that was helping to bring the Hong Kong mafia to justice.

Maritime terrorism and smuggling were two of the Navy's prime targets for the 1990s, the First Sea Lord had said – and nowhere in the world, perhaps, were these problems more acute than the waters around the Crown Colony.

Lately the repatriation of Vietnamese refugees and British citizenship for Chinese residents after 1997 had taken up the headlines – but meanwhile the day-to-day struggle to contain the rising tide of organised crime continued to keep the Hong Kong Squadron's three remaining patrol craft working at full stretch.

In the previous year HMS Starling alone made dozens of arrests, recovering over five million Hong Kong dollars worth of smuggled goods.

The Triad gangsters who control the rackets once thought they had found a way to evade arrest by racing though shallow waters where the big police launches could not follow. But the Squadron countered with Sea Riders – rigid inflatables with a speed of 50 knots plus – and in the first three months of operation caught up with 24 cargoes of contraband.

TV sets were a popular item – but sometimes the haul was more sinister. The drugs trade remained as keen as ever and the Triads made a bit of money on the side by providing transport for illegal immigrants from mainland China. At extortionate rates, with, needless to say, no guarantee for safe delivery.

Despite new laws making it a criminal offence for "IIs" to live or work in Hong Kong, with prison terms of up to 15 months meted out to offenders, the traffic went on. Each patrol craft carried out around 500 boardings a year, checking for stowaways as well as other dubious shipments. [*February 1990*]

208

209

210

210 Storm-swept Guzz

Patrol boats HMS Sandpiper and HMS Petrel are too close for comfort as Devonport is swept by its worst recorded storm. They were berthed alongside each other on the sea wall next to No 4 Basin and the two ship's companies were long engaged in a desperate struggle to keep them from battering each other as winds gusted up to 100 mph.

Here, a floating crane tied alongside the Royal Marines training ship Messina broke adrift and was blown onto a small RMAS vessel, which started to take in water and had to be pumped out.

Alongside No 3 Wharf the Type 21 frigate HMS Alacrity took a heavy buffeting, while as the gales swept Plymouth Sound the Type 22 frigates HMS Sheffield and HMS Battleaxe dragged their anchors and were forced to take to the open sea.

At Torpoint the RFA Argus threatened to part her mooring lines and six RMAS tugs were needed to keep her in position.

The frigate complex was evacuated when a large section of the roof blew off. Throughout the Dockyard roads were closed and traffic diverted as roofing materials and masonry rained down.

Other naval bases escaped relatively lightly – but at Portsmouth the 100ft aircraft lighter RNAL 54, under tow on her way to refit at Devonport, was blown ashore when the hawser snapped and beached below Southsea Castle. As the strong winds continued, it was four days before she could be taken off. [*March 1990*]

211

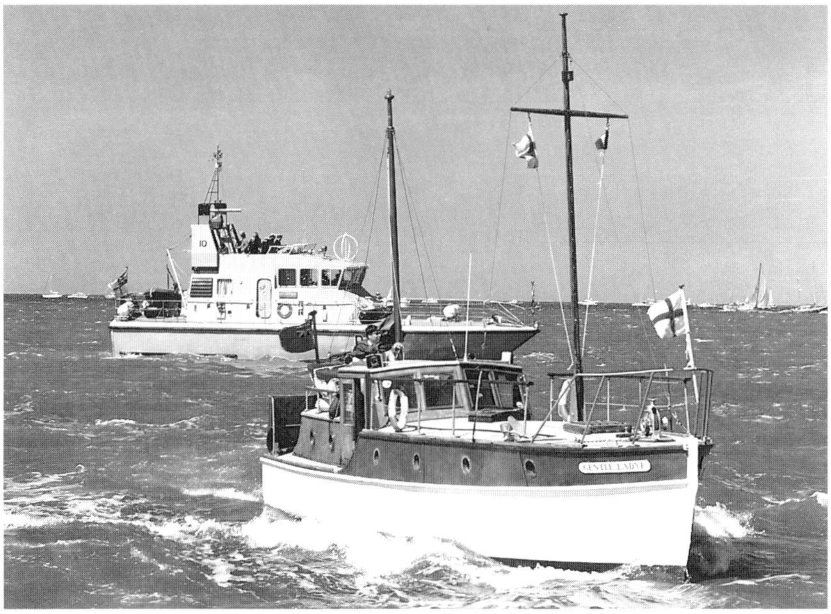

211 Little ships, big hearts

The RNR fast training boat HMS Trumpeter provides an escort for the cabin cruiser Gentle Ladye, one of the original "little ships" that responded to the call to take part in the evacuation of Dunkirk 50 years before.

They did not have to dodge any dive

bombers – this time the Channel itself turned nasty. Part of the miracle of Dunkirk was the flat calm that lasted for 11 days in the Spring of 1940. But when over 70 vessels set out again to retrace their voyage of deliverance there were heavy seas and a brisk northeasterly to battle against.

Several small craft had to return to harbour – but the majority made it across the 35 miles from Dover carefully shepherded by the Type 21 frigate HMS Alacrity, the minesweeper HMS Ledbury and Trumpeter and her sisters Puncher and Example.

Many of them were flat-bottomed river craft that had never been meant to go to sea in the first place. And after years of gentle cruising along rivers and estuaries the buffeting they took in crossing one of the world's busiest waterways did them no good at all.

In several cases hardening of the arteries led to heart failure – fuel lines clogged by the sludge stirred up from the bottom of tanks caused engines to break down.

The RN ships' divers were among those willing hands that worked overtime to keep the miniature armada more or less intact as it slowly retraced the path of the evacuation of 340,000 British and Allied troops that was truly a victory in defeat.

During the Whitsun Bank Holiday week-end 3,000 of the men they saved marched through the centre of Dunkirk and attended a service on the beach where once they had waited under fire before wading waist-deep out to the boats – now formed in a large semicircle half a mile off shore. [*July 1990*]

212

212 **Cardiff pulls Penang honours**

"Three cheers for His Majesty Duli Yang Maha Mulia Sezi Paduka Badinga Yang Dipertuan Agong Sultan Azlan Shah... Too late, lads – we've gone past him now!"

Fortunately it was not necessary to call the Sultan of Malaysia by name when HMS Cardiff saluted him at his International Royal Fleet Review.

And far from disgracing herself among the 60 ships representing 22 navies gathered for the occasion at Penang, the Type 42 destroyer came out on top in the attendant sports events.

After marching through the city with the Royal Marines Band of the Royal Yatch, the ship's company beat the USA and the USSR to win the tug-of-war and came third in the golf tournament.

An even more creditable third placing was gained in such eastern specialities as trishaw and dragon boat racing – in the latter Thailand beat the RN team to second place by just 0.4 of a second while Singapore was more comfortably first across the line a quarter of a minute ahead. [*July 1990*]

213 **Seven year itch scratched**

FLOTEX 90 provided the rare sight of all classes of mine countermeasures vessels exercising together. Ships of the 1st, 3rd, 4th and 10th Squadrons tackled a full and varied training programme – in which HMS Sheraton, the old lady of the group, won the annual Minehunting Efficiency Trophy.

Later there was a friendly meeting of old adversaries when five ships of the 10th visited Esbjerg, Denmark. There Lieut.-Cdr Adrian Legge RNR, in command of the Mersey Division's HMS Ribble, invited on board Captain Kent Kirk, the Danish Minister of Fisheries. They had last met over seven years earlier – when Legge arrested him in a well-publicised infringement of British fishery limits. [*September 1990*]

213

214

214 Package deal

As HMS Fearless (right) held her Families Day off Spithead she met up with her sister HMS Intrepid – a rare chance for two old ladies to be seen together at sea. The two amphibious assault ships – Fearless was fresh out of refit and newly re-commissioned – were among the longest-serving units of the Fleet. Fearless had spent two years at Devonport Dockyard after being decommissioned for three. The work package was the biggest the dockyard had handled since completion of the carrier HMS Invincible and cost £50m. [*January 1991*]

JACK
BY TUGG
.... SHE HAS NOT HEARD FROM YOU FOR OVER A MONTH AND IS FRANTIC WITH WORRY
WHAT'S YOUR EXCUSE?
IF I COULD THINK OF A GOOD ONE SIR – I'D 'AVE WRITTEN TO 'ER

215

216

215 Raising the flag

The minesweeper HMS Hurworth's Gulf War battle ensign is hoisted by RO Mike Dawson as she prepares to counter the Iraqi mine threat. [*February 1991*]

216 Wise sisters under the sun

HMS Minerva (rear) met up with her NATO namesake, an Italian corvette, while operating in the Mediterranean in support of Operation Desert Storm. The RN frigate had also been continuing her role as a member of the Dartmouth Training Squadron, with visits to Gibraltar, La Spezia, Barcelona and Toulon. [*April 1991*]

217

217 Paint job for a pair of O-boats

HMS Otus enters Haslar Creek, Gosport flying her Jolly Roger and covered in camouflage paint – her sister Opossum had preceded her in the same style a few days before – causing speculation over cloak-and-dagger operations in the Gulf. She was also flying her paying off pennant to mark the end of 28 years' service so it seemed her swan song sounded a note of glory... The paintwork, in duck egg blue and black, had been applied in much the same pattern as that adopted by British submarines in the Far East in 1943–45 – though shades of light and dark green were then favoured in operations against the Japanese.

HMS Opossum had returned from a rare (for a submarine) round-the-world deployment which began in May the previous year and took her to Pitcairn Island – where she joined the 200th anniversary of the Bounty mutineers' settlement – Tahiti, Australia, Java and Singapore. [*May 1991*]

218 In another part of the forest

HMS Charybdis steams smartly away from HMS Ark Royal and the guided missile cruiser USS Virginia after a multi-national serial in the Eastern Mediterranean. The Ark had been leading Task Group 323.2 – HMS Manchester and Sheffield and the RFAs Olmeda and Regent – operating in support of US Navy units backing Desert Storm. The Manchester was called forward to join the Gulf Task Group and was replaced by HMS Charybdis, which helped to continue a useful series of exercises with other NATO ships, including a joint air defence exercise in the Ionian Sea involving 18 ships from seven NATO countries. [*May 1991*]

218

219

219 Unseen in the foreground

The Liverpool skyline forms a backdrop for the second of the Type 2400 patrol submarines HMS Unseen, operating from Birkenhead on contractor's sea trials.

Completion of these coincided with a big day for the third of class, HMS Ursula, with the Unseen back in the Mersey to salute the launch of her sister sub. [*May 1991*]

220 Agony of the Kurds

A Sea King from 846 Sqn lands at a Kurdish refugee camp in northern Iraq. Operation Haven brought in the Royal Marines to protect a tide of humanity that represented the world's largest stateless nation, fleeing from the armies of Saddam Hussein and now suffering at the hands of bandits. The Allied forces provided the only law and order in a country overrun by guerrillas and thieves who were quick to spirit away air-dropped relief supplies that chanced to drift just a short way from the camps. Most dangerous of all, however, was the risk of epidemics. Wren PO Mary Norris, serving with the Navy Medical team, told Navy News every child she had seen was affected by diarrhoea, rickets or scabies. Nearly 70 per cent of the child deaths were under fives. [*June 1991*]

221

221 Assault on a maidenhead

On arrival in the British Virgin Islands HMS Fearless launched a dawn assault on Beef Island – with the Governor's permission. Her Rigid Raiders are seen here leaving "mother" for picturesque Long Bay beach, where the fourth Assault Squadron was able to set up an operations base in record time. [*July 1991*]

222 Arrow shoots another line of cocaine

Returning from the South Atlantic, the Type 21 frigate HMS Arrow – seen here with the US Coastguard patrol boat Point Thatcher – played a major role in a dramatic drug seizure in the Caribbean. While carrying out anti-drug trafficking patrols off the Bahamas, Arrow picked up a suspect aircraft track on her long distance air defence radar and immediately relayed the information to the Coastguard, who directed their helicopters to intercept.

HMS Arrow continued to monitor the aircraft's progress to its landing site on Acklins Island. The Coastguard helicopters flew in and picked up 1,500lb of cocaine, though the smugglers managed to evade arrest. [*August 1991*]

220

222

223

224

223 **Russian Roulette**

Events in Russia led to a halt in plans for HMS London to make a commemorative visit to Murmansk to mark the 50th anniversary of the first Arctic convoy. Together with RFA Tidespring, the Type 22 frigate had a role in what were to have been the first RN/Soviet exercises since the Second World War, with veterans from several nations invited to watch and attend ceremonies in North Russia.

An attempted coup by a hard-line junta brought tanks into the centre of Moscow – but in the event Operation Dervish 91 was allowed to go ahead.

Dervish had been the code name for the original convoy – now re-enacted to rousing cheers from RN and Soviet sailors as eleven naval, merchant and salvage vessels formed up in the Barents Sea.

Soviet fighters and bombers flew overhead bombarding the ships with dummy ordnance and as submarine-launched drill torpedoes skimmed between the convoy vessels one PO on board HMS London was heard to remark: "These guys would frighten the life out of the Sea Training staff at Portland..." As a young man, Admiral Vladimir Mikhailin (76), now Chairman of the Soviet Veterans Committee, commanded one of the three British minesweepers given to Russia by Churchill.

His ship, Minesweeper 1110, won the Order of the Red Banner, the highest Soviet military award, for destroying 41 German mines – and he remembered with fondness the three barrels of rum left on board by the minesweeper's delivery crew.

● The Kirov class cruiser Kalinin was earlier photographed in the North Sea in company with HMS Brazen. [*September 1991*)

224 **Fearless in Sevastopol**

Sevastopol, the Ukrainian capital of the Crimea and home of the Soviet Navy's Black Sea Fleet, had not seen a British warship in harbour for over 40 years, a period which encompassed the dark days of the Cold War – and more recent astounding changes as the effects of Perestroika and Glasnost had been felt.

HMS Fearless's visit, part of a continuing build-up of stronger ties between the Royal and former Soviet Navies, came at a time of growing uncertainty, however, with the prospect of the old Soviet Union fragmenting and Ukrainian nationalists wanting to set up their own forces and take over the Black Sea Fleet.

But none of this tension interfered with the warmth and openness of the British visitors' welcome.

When Fearless was open to visitors the crowds were so huge that Soviet sailors had to be brought in to hold them back. Many local families took crew members, male and female, into their homes – a supremely generous gesture, given the shortages that were painfully apparent in the shops.

LS Steve Dermott rated Sevastopol highly as a run ashore: "There were fourteen of us. We had a two course meal, bottles of wine, vodka and champagne. The bill for the lot came to £4."

Most remarkably, Sevastopol had hitherto been a closed military city – for most Soviet citizens it was unknown territory, with its borders guarded and access restricted.

Rear Admiral Bruce Richardson, flying his flag in Fearless, was paying his second recent visit to the Soviet Union – he had been to Murmansk in HMS London in September.

"The Soviets opened up their warships, their aircraft, their homes and their hearts to us," he commented. [*December 1991*]

225 **No let up for Hermione**

HMS Hermione on patrol in the Gulf. Further military expansion by Iran was giving a new edge to the Royal Navy's presence there – still facing a continuing threat from Iraq.

A year after the Gulf War mines remained a danger. There were still sunken ships and defensive mines at the entrances to Iraq's waterways – but at the same time no trade was passing to Iraq through the Gulf as United Nations sanctions continued. [*February 1992*]

225

226

226 *Thin on top*

Nukes on top of the world again – HMS Trenchant meets up with USS Spadefish for a now regular rendezvous at the North Pole.

The ice where they cut through was too thin to allow the usual games of cricket and baseball – nothing to do with global warming, though... [*June 1992*]

227 *Summit meeting*

As Rio de Janeiro prepared to host the Earth Summit, HMS Campbeltown sailed in for a six day visit. The Type 22 frigate is seen here on departure, passing Sugar Loaf Mountain. [*July 1992*]

227

JACK
By TUGG.
..the reason I haven't written is dead simple.......

228 *Off to the Orient*

A Sea King from 845 Naval Air Squadron watches over the Orient 92 Task Group off Gibraltar. HMS Invincible, with HMS Norfolk, HMS Newcastle and HMS Boxer, sustained by RFA Fort Austin, were off on a seven month deployment to the Far East, by the end of which they would have steamed 25,000 miles and visited 29 ports in 20 countries. [*September 1992*]

229, 230 *The Andrew after Andrew*

When Eleuthera and the Berry Islands in the Bahamas were devastated by Hurricane Andrew, HMS Cardiff (pictured here off Eleuthera with (inset) the ravaged northern part of the island) was joined by RFA Orangeleaf and HMS Campbeltown in response to an appeal for aid.

Within five hours working parties were being put ashore with water, food and medical assistance. The devastation was widespread, with many homes flattened, power supplies damaged and water filtration and sewage plants knocked out. On Harbour Island not a single building escaped.

The Royal Navy's $1m relief effort was completed in a week – after which Cardiff moved on to Nassau while Campbeltown continued her voyage home from the Falklands. [*October 1992*]

228

229, 230

231

231 Trident on trial in the Vanguard

Escorted by the offshore patrol vessel HMS Orkney, the first of the UK's Trident submarines HMS Vanguard was making her way to the Clyde submarine base to begin her trials.

Defence Secretary Malcolm Rifkind commented: "The Cold War has ended but we still live in an uncertain and unstable world. Now, more than ever, it is vital to retain Trident."

232

232 The White Company

A Sea King from 845 Naval Air Squadron – for the first time in white United Nations livery – tests anti-missile decoy flares over RFA Argus as she nears the Croation port of Split.

The Type 42 destroyer HMS Gloucester was also standing by to protect her – but the Argus's sole mission was to provide casualty evacuation in case members of the Cheshire Regiment were caught in the bitter fighting in Bosnia.

She was not to be used to carry troops or military supplies. A multi-national flotilla of warships was starting a full-scale oil blockade against Serbia in the Adriatic.

233 Merlin defies the elements

Gale force winds and rough seas faced the EH101 Merlin, the new anti-submarine warfare helicopter for the Royal Navy, as it teamed up with HMS Iron Duke for ship handling trials in the Channel. In 40-50 knot winds above 20ft waves the aircraft made 69 landings on the Type 23 frigate – visited around this time by the Duke of Wellington, whose famous forebear's nickname she bears. [*April 1993*]

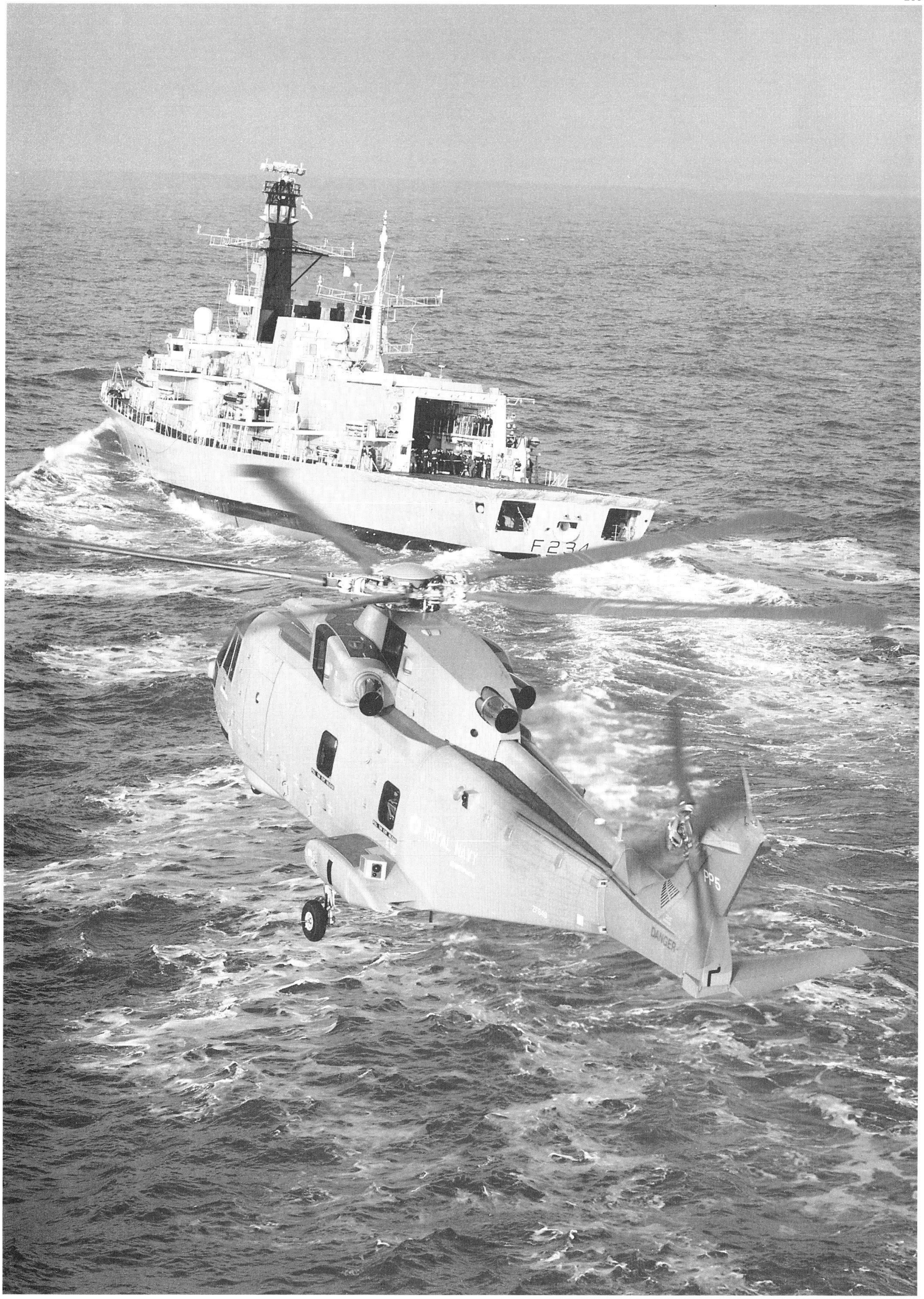
F234
ROYAL NAVY
PP5
DANGER

234

234 **Hurworth stands down**
Mine countermeasures vessel HMS Hurworth leads the Standing Naval Force Channel at the end of a year which had kept her at sea for 150 days and taken her to 25 European ports. These had included Gdynia in Poland, Klaipeda in Lithuania and Riga in Latvia. Command of the NATO force was about to be handed over to the Netherlands. [*July 1993*]

235

235 *Atlantic squall*

HMS Liverpool, in relatively calm waters with ships of the international fleet off Anglesey, rehearsing for the Battle of the Atlantic 50th anniversary Fleet Review – which was visited by Force 8 winds.

The Duke of Edinburgh and King Harald of Norway were embarked in HMY Britannia for the review of 26 warships and seven merchant vessels, carried out, in the end, in "real Battle of the Atlantic weather" which many of the veterans embarked remembered only too well.

A number of smaller vessels were forced to withdraw – but one of the smallest to survive the battering, HMS Humber, Commodore RNR, managed to stay in line throughout.

The commemorations centred on Liverpool, nerve centre of the battle which saw its turning point in May, 1943 as the home of the Western Approaches Combined Headquarters.

Over 3,000 veterans took part in a parade through the city centre – the biggest march-past organised by the Navy since World War II.

Among the Royal visitors to the city were the Prince and Princess of Wales, who attended a service at the Anglican Cathedral. [*July 1993*]

236 *Triumphal progress*

Looking a bit weather-beaten on her arrival at HMAS Stirling is HMS Triumph, the first RN nuclear-powered submarine to visit Australia.

She was making a record-breaking 46,700 mile voyage to demonstrate how far nuclear submarines could operate without surface support – and the Royal Navy's role in 'power projection' into the next century.

When she returned to Devonport she had been away for 197 days – 151 of them at sea and 131 of those dived – with well-earned breaks at Gibraltar, Abu Dhabi, Diego Garcia, Perth and Singapore.

Taking part in exercises with RN ships and naval vessels from a number of friendly countries, she operated in the Atlantic Ocean, off the Cape of Good Hope, in the Southern Indian Ocean, the Arabian Sea, Gulf of Oman, Straits of Hormuz, Arabian Gulf, Sunda Strait, Java Sea, South China Sea, Singapore Straits, Malacca Straits, Mediterranean and Straits of Gibraltar.

She was the first nuclear-powered submarine to operate in the Gulf. [*August 1993*]

236

237

239

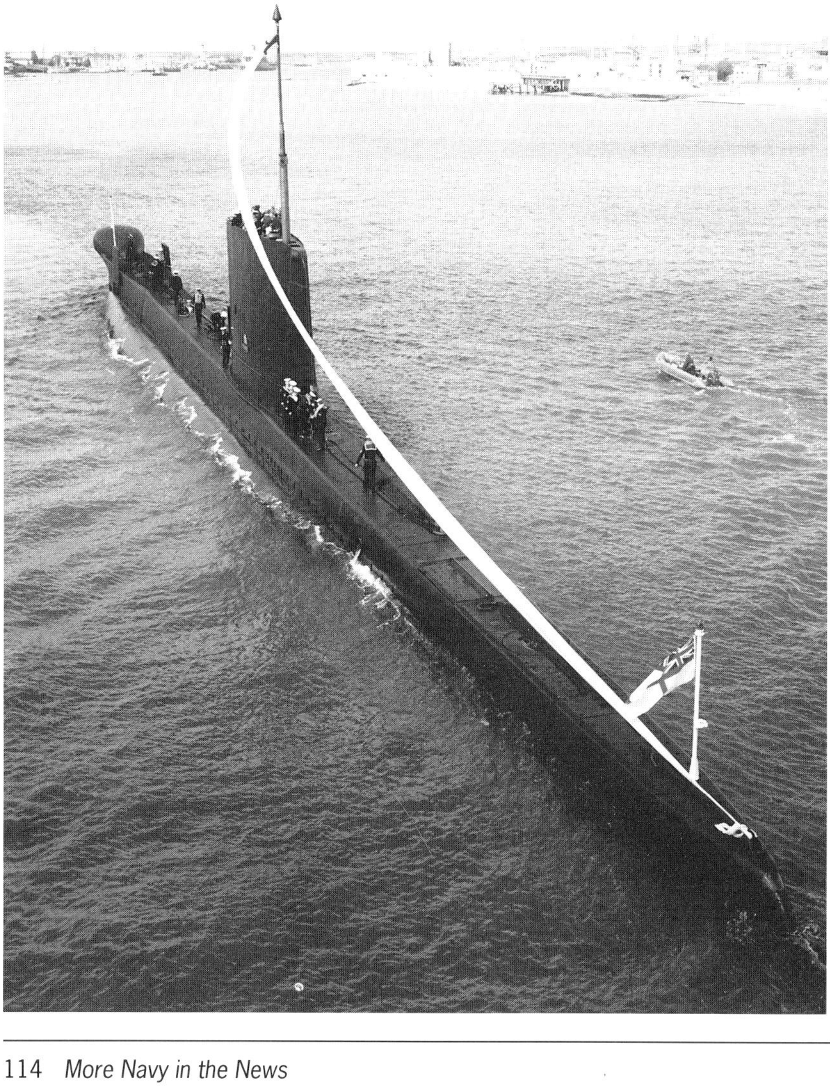

237 Leaders in Europe

Ten Lynx aircraft from 815 Naval Air Squadron at Portland in a formation fly-past to celebrate a successful first term as Europe's largest helicopter squadron. [*September 1993*]

238 Russ plugs in

Lieut. Russ Eatwell successfully plugs in for fuel – 800 Naval Air Squadron's Sea Harriers were this month operating from HMS Invincible in the Adriatic, ready to support UN forces ashore in Bosnia.

The photographer got his thumb in the way, though... [*October 1993*]

239 'Possum plays out

Flying her paying off pennant at the end of her 30-year career, HMS Opossum, last of the Oberon class diesel-electric submarines, makes her final run into HMS Dolphin – where she also marked the end of 90 years' continuous submarine operation out of Gosport. [*October 1993*]

238

240

240 **Boxer – by Canaletto?**
Looking like a modern version of a painting by Canaletto is HMS Boxer, visiting Venice for a two-week maintenance period. She had been taking part in exercises with USS Simpson and carrying out her duties as part of the UK task force patrolling the coast of the former Yugoslavia.

In commemoration of the 50th anniversary of the Allied landings in Italy, the Type 22 frigate also visited Salerno to take part in a wreath laying ceremony at sea. [*November 1993*]

241

243

241 Knights in white armour

Wearing white United Nations livery, four Sea Kings of 845 Naval Air Squadron fly low into their base at the Croatian port of Split.

By this time 845 was the UN's longest-serving unit in the war zone of the former Yugoslavia, having conducted a year-long mercy mission in a harsh and dangerous environment.

Some of the squadron's successes had been achieved under fire and they were always under threat of it.

Their bravery had been recognised by awards in the Queen's Birthday Honours List – of the Air Force Cross to 845's commanding officer, Lt Cdr George Wallace; the Queen's Commendation for Valuable Service in the Air to Lt Kevin Smith; and a Mention in Despatches for Lt Tim Kelly.

These had resulted from the evacuation of Muslim refugees from the besieged town of Srebrenica. [*December 1993*]

JACK
YOU KNOW THAT BIG EXPENSIVE VALENTINE CARD I GOT – WITH THE RIBBON, AN' GOLD AN' RED ROSES? – I SENT IT TO THAT WREN IN THE CAPTAIN'S OFFICE
I KNOW. I WATCHED HER PUT IT IN THE SHREDDER.

242

242 **Royal date for Lancaster**

The Duke Class Type 23 frigate HMS Lancaster cuts a dash as she steams up the Thames to keep an appointment with the Queen.

Her Majesty, who launched the Type 23 frigate in 1990 (one of the Queen's titles is Duke of Lancaster) called on the ship when she tied up at Canary Wharf. [*January 1994*]

243 **'Further South' with Endurance**

HMS Endurance travelled further south into the Antarctic pack ice than any other RN ship when she reached 77° 27'S 34° 02'W in the Weddell Sea – just 735 miles from the South Pole.

By coincidence she had closely followed the track of Sir Ernest Shackleton's Endurance 79 years before.

She passed close to the position (76° 34'S 31 30'W) where Shackleton's ship was beset in the ice on 18 January 1915. The old Endurance had then drifted SW to reach the 77th parallel at 35° W four days before being carried NW by the floe. She was eventually crushed and sank on November 21 that same year.

The purpose of the Navy's Ice Patrol Ship's expedition this time had been to support the British Antarctic Survey in setting up a depot as close as possible to the Shackleton Mountains in preparation for the following year's international geological survey project Euroshack.

This would investigate the tectonic plate theory – that the Shackleton range was once joined to Texas, USA. [*May 1994*]

Index of ships

Printed in the United Kingdom for HMSO
Dd 296877 C40 6/94 3400/1 12521